MW00695405

Unless otherwise noted, all scriptural citations are from the New King James Translations 1990, 1985, 1983, Thomas Nelson, Nashville, Tn.

9780965380492

Produced by JaDon Management Inc.
1405 4th Ave. N. W. #109
Ardmore, Ok. 73401

The purpose of this book is:

1.) To teach and defend the integrity and reliability of God,

2.) To teach and defend the Deity of Jesus Christ,

3.) To teach and defend the inspiration of the Bible, by demonstrating that God has fulfilled *all* His prophetic Word.

THE LAST DAYS: IDENTIFIED!

By Don K. PRESTON
With contributions by John Anderson

Foreword

The tragic events of 9-11 as documented by *Time* magazine, July 1, 2002, created a tremendous interest in the study of the "last days." People want to know what the future holds, and how it will all "end." That interest has led to the sale of an incredible 62+ million copies of the *Left Behind* books, the fictionalized version of Biblical eschatology (the study of last things), as envisioned by the late Tim LaHaye. There are thousands, if not millions, of people who believe that earth is in its last days.

Is this what the Bible says? Are the events depicted in the *Left Behind* books and movies just around the corner, or are those books fiction after all? I am convinced that the *Left Behind* books are in fact, fictional, with no basis in the Bible at all!

No study of "last things" is more important than the study of the "last days." Modern prophecy pundits like LaHaye confidently proclaim that we are indeed in the last days, that no other generation has ever seen the signs of the end like ours. Of course, they conveniently overlook the fact that every generation has claimed the identical thing! Passages that speak of the last days are read, and applied with confidence to newspaper headlines, as if there is little doubt that the last time is *now*!

What if we are *not* in the last days? What if the Bible defines the "last days" as a time unrelated to our modern world? What if it could be *proven* that the last days have already come and gone? That is what this book is about. I am convinced that the "last days" are past, and that they passed with the end of the Old Covenant World of Israel in AD 70.

Inspiration for this book came from two sources. In 1997, I helped organize a prophecy conference in Oklahoma City. My friend William Bell spoke on the "last days." His lesson was so logical and thorough that it convinced me that something needed to be done in book form. Other projects however, took precedence. Then, my friend, the late John Anderson shared some thoughts on Genesis 49 with me. At first, what he said did not strike me with the same conviction that John obviously held. However, his patience and persistence paid off. As I began the research, it dawned on me what John was trying to get me to see. The lights came on. Finally, it was time to write a book on the "last days." My thanks to John for his contributions to this book.

This book will prove that we are not in the Biblical last days. And for that, we can all be thankful.   **Don K. Preston (D. Div.)**

ARE WE IN THE LAST DAYS?

"The Last Days." The term sounds ominous, threatening. It indicates that something is ending. In the Bible, the term "last days" is important, because at the close of the last days, God would bring His scheme of redemption to its consummation. Many believe that the end of human history, and the destruction (or at least cataclysmic purging), of the physical universe is associated with the close of the last days, and that it is near.

On the millennial website www.prophecy.com we find this statement, "Our position is 'Pre-Trib.' We agree with Bible teachers like Chuck Missler, Chuck Smith, Hal Lindsey, J.R. Church, Jack Van Impe and a host of other popular and scholarly teachers who believe that we are living in 'The Last Days,' and can expect to see Christ return in our generation. We don't believe in setting dates for His return, but believe it will be soon." This kind of thinking permeates the modern evangelical community. The wildly popular *Left Behind* books and movies have thousands, if not millions, of people convinced that "the end is near."

Just what are the last days? How does the Bible actually define the term? It will surprise you to know that the Bible teaches something very different than most prophecy pundits.

This book will help you determine for yourself, from the Bible, the proper definition of the last days. Further, when you realize the correct definition of the last days, you will discover a very positive view of the future. You will be able to live in confidence. Just as the bumper stickers proclaim "No Fear!," the proper understanding of the last days will allow you to "cast out fear," and face the future with assurance.

There is no issue more important to the study of eschatology, i.e. the study of last things, than the identity of the last days.[1] Lots of folks talk about the anti-Christ, the Man of Sin, the Mark of the Beast, etc.. And, if we are in the last days, then surely, the modern prophecy pundits are correct that the end is near, and these frightening entities are a coming reality. If however, we are not in the last days, all of the current excitement caused by the *Left Behind* books and movies is misplaced, and, in fact, is a disservice to Christianity.

Make no mistake about the importance of this book. Our purpose is to demonstrate, through scripture alone, that when the Bible speaks of the last days, that it refers to the last days of the Old Covenant World of Israel that came to an end with the fall of Jerusalem in A.D. 70. We will show that the Christian Age is not the last days. We will show that the Bible does not predict the end of time.

If we can show, and I am confident we can, that the Bible term "the last days," does not refer to the end of time, or the end of the Christian Age, but to the last days of Old Covenant Israel, the implications for all futurist eschatologies are devastating. To demonstrate that we are not in the last days, and that the last days are not in the future, falsifies the eschatological system of the Amillennialists, the premillennialists and the post-millennialists. It falsifies the Adventist movement, the Latter Day Saints Movement, the Anglo-Israelism movement, the Jehovah's Witness Movement, and all apocalyptic movements that proclaim that we are in the last days. This is the importance of properly identifying the last days.

So, what are the last days? There are basically three differing definitions offered by the varying schools of futurist eschatology.

First, we are told that the last days is referent to the entirety of the Christian era. The last days supposedly began on Pentecost, in A. D. 33, and will end with the second coming of Christ, at the end of time. That means that the last days have lasted so far 2000 years. This is the view of most Amillennialists and Postmillennialists. Kenneth Gentry summarizes the amillennial and postmillennial view, "The postmillennial view of the 'last days' is that the last days of the Old Covenant era introduced the great era of historical victory for the Church of Jesus Christ."[2] In other words, the last days of the Jewish Age introduced the last days, i.e. the Christian Age.

Second, the last days are defined by the millennialists as the 70th week of Daniel 9. This critical 7 year period of time refers to the time initiated by the Rapture, or more specifically, the time beginning with the signing of the peace treaty with the Anti-Christ. This last days of Israel is thus seen as future, and of only 7 years duration. However, it should be noted that the millennialists also believe that the term last days *in the New Testament* refers to the last days of the Christian Age. Ice says, "We must distinguish between the 'last days' of the Church Age, and the 'last days' of Israel's tribulation."[3] We must also note that in a radio debate I had with Thomas Ice he said that the *entire Christian Age* is called the "last days." Thus, the millennialists, at least in some cases, believe the term "last days" has no less than *three* Biblical definitions, and they all refer to different, even contrasting ideas.

Third, the term "the last days" is defined as the last generation of Israel's Old Covenant Age that ended in Christ's coming in A. D. 70.

As you can see, most definitions of the last days are applied to the present or future. The *entire Christian Age* is called the last days. The *last generation of the Christian Age* is called the last days, and a yet future 7 year period consummating Israel's Age is called the last days.

Note that all three futurists views claim that the Bible uses the term "the last days" to refer to both *a short period of time*, i.e. the closing generation of the Old Covenant World of Israel, as well as the entirety of the Christian

Age. This means of course, that the same term is being defined in two totally different, and contrasting ways.

This book will prove that the Bible knows of only one "last days" period, and that this is a referent, not to the end of human history, or the Christian Age, but to the end of the Old Covenant World of Israel that occurred with the fall of Jerusalem in A.D. 70.

A note or two on our method in this book. My normal style is to offer extensive bibliographic references. However, for brevity sake, I will keep my references to a minimum. Further, there are some passages that mention the last days that do not directly contribute to our ability to properly define the *framework* of the last days. In the cases where the information is sparse, we will not examine the texts. We will focus our attention on those passages that give us the most defining information. Information that can serve as a "nail" on which to hang our hat, so to speak. In this way, this book can be kept to a smaller format, and be the most beneficial to the reader. Let us begin our investigation of the "last days" with the first mention of the term in the Bible.

GENESIS 49:1-10

As the patriarch Jacob entered his "last days" he gathered his sons around him to give them a prophetic blessing: "Gather together, that I may tell you what shall befall you in the last days." Then, for our study, we find a particularly significant verse: "The scepter shall not depart from Judah, nor a lawgiver from between his feet, until Shiloh comes, and to him shall be the obedience of the people." (v. 10)

There are several constituent elements of this prophecy.

1.) The focus, i.e. the sons of Jacob. This means it is not about the end of the Church Age, it is about *the last days of Israel*.

2.) The time frame– the topic of our study, **the last days**.

3.) The passing of the scepter from Judah.

4.) The coming of Shiloh, or Messiah in his kingdom.

5.) The gathering of the people to him.

The topic is not the church, nor the Church Age, yet the topic is what would happen in the last days. Thus, in the first occurrence of the term "last days," in an eschatological context, the term has nothing to do with the Christian Age. *It deals with the fate of Israel!*

Notice again that Jacob made a promise to his sons, and specifically Judah: "The scepter shall not depart from Judah nor a lawgiver from between his feet, until Shiloh comes and to him shall be the obedience of the people."

There is a fascinatingly similar passage found in Genesis 28:15f concerning the time when God's distinctive relationship with Jacob and his seed would be terminated:

"I am the Lord God of Abraham your father and the God of Isaac; the land on which you lie I will give to you and your descendants. Also your descendants shall be as the dust of the earth; you shall spread abroad to the west and the east, to the north and the south; and in you and in your seed all the families of the earth shall be blessed. Behold, I am with you and will keep you where ever you go, and will bring you back to this land; for I will not leave you until I have done what I have spoken to you."

This passage cannot be speaking of Jacob individually. It is a reiteration of the Abrahamic and Messianic Covenant. Like Genesis 49, it indicates that when Jehovah had fulfilled His promises to the seed of Abraham, to Israel, that the distinctive and exclusive relationship would then be terminated.

What we have in Genesis 49 specifically is that Judah would remain the focal point of the theocracy *until the appointed Messiah would come*. We need to take a closer look at this important text.

A "Yahoo" search of the term "Genesis 49:10" resulted in 1500+ articles and sites by Christians, Jews and Muslims on the importance of this passage. All three groups seem to agree that the scepter, the ruling authority, and God's distinctive relationship with Judah ceased with the fall of Jerusalem in A.D. 70.

We need to point out, for clarity sake, that the Babylonian Talmud, in recalling how the authority of capital punishment had been taken from Israel *before* AD 70 lamented: "Woe unto us for the scepter has departed from Judah and the Messiah has not come!"[4] However, even though the general authority of capital punishment had been taken from Judah, there were exceptions,[5] and, more importantly, her national identity, and authority *represented by the Temple,* was not removed until A.D. 70.

Now if the scepter departed from Judah in A.D. 70, for us to maintain a faith in the integrity of scripture, and the faithfulness of the God who cannot lie, we must believe, contra the Jews and Moslems, and, we might add, *the millennialists*, that Messiah did indeed come *in the last days*. And, he came when the scepter was removed from Judah, at the fall of Jerusalem in A.D. 70.

This golden thread of motifs from Genesis 49, the departure of the scepter from Judah, and the establishment of the kingdom of Messiah runs throughout prophecy. In Isaiah 11 we find the prediction of the coming of *the root of Jesse*. This is *Shiloh* of the tribe of Judah. His reign is described in verses 1-9, and note particularly v. 9, "They shall not hurt nor destroy in my holy mountain." This verse is quoted again, *verbatim*, in chapter 65:25. We need then to examine Isaiah 65 more closely, because it contains the motifs of Genesis 49 that demand our attention.

First, Israel would fill the measure of her sin (v. 6). Note that it says, "Your sins, and the sins of your fathers will I measure into your bosom." The collective sins of Israel would finally catch up to them. We do not have to wonder when this would be. In Matthew 23, Jesus said Israel would fill up the measure of her sin in his generation. Paul, circa A.D. 50, added that Israel was filling up the measure of her sin by persecuting God's elect (1 Thessalonians 2:15f). John added that the enigmatic city Babylon, "where the Lord was slain," had filled up the measure of her sin and was about to be destroyed (Revelation 11, 18:20, 24).[6]

Second, Israel would be destroyed, "The Lord God will slay you!"(v. 13f). This was spoken to *Old Covenant Israel*. This is another way of saying the scepter would depart from Judah. Thus, the term "last days" agrees with the idea that when Jehovah had fulfilled His purposes, the temporary, external form would pass away. When Israel entered her "last days," *when Jesus arrived* (Hebrews 1:1), it signaled both *bad news*, the dissolution of the Old Covenant form, and *good news*, the establishment of the New Creation.

Third, a new people would be created (v. 13f). The Old Covenant form of Israel was not intended by Jehovah to be eternal. It was a shadow of good things to come.[7]

Fourth, the New Heaven and Earth would be created (v. 17f). It is clear from the text, but sadly, most commentators seem to miss it, that the promised New Creation is a *Covenant World*. Note that Jehovah would create this New Order only when Israel was destroyed, *when the scepter was removed from Judah*. Further, when the New Heavens and Earth was created, "the former (*the former heavens and earth*, DKP), will no longer be remembered" (v. 17).

Charles Spurgeon posed the following questions and thoughts,
"Did you ever regret the absence of the burnt-offering, or the red heifer, or any of the sacrifices and rites of the Jews? Did you ever pine for the feast of Tabernacles, or dedication? No, because, though these were like the old heavens and earth to the Jewish believers, they have passed away, and we now live under new heavens and earth, so far as the dispensation of divine teaching is concerned. The substance is come, and the shadow has gone: and we do not remember it"[8]

While Spurgeon maintained a futurist eschatology, he nonetheless saw, to some degree, the significance of the passing of the Old World of Israel. He saw that the dissolution of Israel's national form led to the New Heaven and Earth of Jesus Christ.

I do not know of *anyone* that believes that God will destroy literal heaven and earth because Israel will fill up the measure of her sin, and then create another literal New Creation. Yet, Isaiah predicted that when Israel filled the measure of her sin, and was destroyed, that Jehovah would destroy heaven and earth, create a new people, and create a New Heavens and Earth. This is dealing with the last days of Israel, not promises to the church at the end of time.

The important thing to remember here is the association with Genesis 49. Isaiah agrees perfectly with Genesis, that at the time when Judah would lose her authority, the kingdom would come. Further, as we have seen, Jesus, Paul and John all agree in placing the fulfillment of Isaiah, the filling up of the measure of Israel's sin, in their generation, consummating in the fall of Jerusalem.

The prophecy of the New Creation cannot be divorced from the time of the judgment of Israel. The Amillennialist and Postmillennialist place the New Heavens and Earth *at the end of the Christian Age, but this is not where inspiration places it.* If the New Creation does not come until some future time when the Christian Age ends, this means Israel will be destroyed at that time! What is the point to that? Did He not do a good job in A.D. 70? Do these two futurist views posit a yet future restoration of Israel that will allow her to then be destroyed once again? No.

If one places the New Creation at the end of the millennium, per LaHaye,[9] *then Israel will be destroyed at the end of the millennium.* Do the millennialists have a place for the destruction of Israel at the end of the millennium? No!

The New Creation, the kingdom of Messiah, would come in the last days, when the scepter would depart from Judah. (Doesn't the idea of the scepter *departing from Judah* itself indicate that the topic is the *last days of Judah?*) But the scepter would depart from Judah when Jehovah destroyed Israel (Isaiah 65), in A. D. 70.

The destruction of Israel, the passing of the scepter from Judah, and the establishment of Messiah's kingdom go hand in hand. They are inseparable Siamese twins. Unless one is willing to say that the destruction of Israel will occur at the end of the Christian Age, or some future millennium, then the fact that Israel *was* destroyed, and the scepter did depart from Judah in A.D. 70, should force us to define the term *last days* as the last days of national Israel.

The golden thread of Genesis 49 not only runs through Isaiah, it is found in the parables of Jesus as well. In Matthew 21, we find the parable of the vineyard, and the wicked husbandmen. Clearly, this is a prophecy concerning Israel, *not the end of the Church Age.* We cannot fail to note the historical context of this parable. In my estimation, Matthew 21 is a *midrash*, a commentary, on Genesis 49.

First, Jesus had entered the city triumphantly. Incidentally, does not this triumphant entry of Jesus, being hailed as king, son of David, and then the immediate cleansing of the temple, indicate that the time for the scepter to pass from Judah, and the coming of the kingdom was near?

Instead of suggesting the postponement of the kingdom, the actions in Matthew 21 proclaimed that the kingdom was at hand. This is especially true since the millennialists insist that the triumphant entry ended the 69th week of Daniel. If the 69th week was ending, that suggests that the 70th week was about to begin, and this surely indicated that Shiloh was about to come in his kingdom. The scepter was about to pass from Judah!

Second, when he entered the city, Jesus cleansed the temple (v. 18), *the symbol of Judah's sovereignty.* This action sent a powerful message in light of the triumphant entry and his identity as the king. It proclaimed, in living parabolic actions, his sovereign authority. Only the king– *the ruler out of Judah*-- had the right to do what he was doing. In the words of Wright, "His Temple-action was a messianic act of judgment."[10] If Jesus' Temple-action was a Messianic act of judgment, it was the action of Shiloh presaging his coming to remove the scepter from Judah.

Third, Jesus now tells the parable, and as Wright notes, the meaning is clear: "The master, who had sent servants and son alike and seen them all rejected, would come and destroy the tenants, and give the vineyard to others. This refers most naturally to the forthcoming destruction of Jerusalem." (1996, 498). Even the millennial *Bible Knowledge Commentary,* by Walvoord, says the kingdom was taken from Judah in A.D. 70.[11]

What we have in Matthew 21 then, is Jesus, the ruler from Judah, asserting his kingly authority, by cleansing the temple, the symbol of Judah's scepter. He foretold the removal of the scepter from Judah when she was judged for killing the prophets and the Son. It cannot be over-emphasized that the removal of the scepter from Judah and the coming of the Messiah into his kingdom, *per Genesis 49*, was to occur in *the last days of Israel.* Thus, the scepter would be removed from Judah in the last days. But the scepter would be removed from Judah in the judgment of Jerusalem in A.D. 70. *Therefore, the last days of Judah were in A.D. 70.* As we will see, this is extremely important, for if the last days of Israel even existed in AD 70 millennialism is invalidated.

Jesus' next parable is also a commentary on Genesis 49, and further defines and confines the last days.

A man made a wedding for his son, and sent his servants to call those who had been invited to the wedding. The invited guests mistreated the servants sent to them, even killing them. The master then, "sent out his armies, and destroyed those murderers and burned their city" (Matthew 22:7). As Hagner says, "It is virtually impossible for post-70 readers of the Gospel not to see the destruction of Jerusalem alluded to in these words."[12] Walvoord also applies the prediction to A.D. 70: "Jesus had in mind the effect of the nations rejection of Him. God's plans for His Son's millennial reign and the invitation had been extended. But the preaching of John the Baptist, Jesus, and the disciples had been largely ignored. The nation would even kill those extending the offer. Finally, in AD 70 the Roman army would come, kill most of the Jews living in Jerusalem, and destroy the temple." (1984, 71)

This parable agrees perfectly with Genesis 49. Jacob said that in the last days, the sovereignty would be transferred from Judah to the Messiah. Judah would lose her prominent position. And, here in the parable, there is a transference of privilege.

It is interesting that Walvoord says, "Since those who were first invited had rejected the invitation, opportunity was then given to a broader group." Well, this can only mean that *the wedding proceeded*, and a "broader group" than just Israel was invited. There is not one word of a postponement of the wedding. The only change is that the previously privileged invited guests are now cast out, while the "broader group" holds the place of privilege. This is really *very important*, because it lets us know that God did not postpone the kingdom/wedding for 2000 years!

Here is the point. Genesis 49 predicted the coming of Messiah into his kingdom, *in the last days of the sons of Jacob*, "I will tell you what shall befall *you* in the last days." This is, of course, the time of the wedding. But Genesis says that at the time of the Messiah's kingdom, *the scepter would pass from Judah*. In Matthew, Jesus has appeared and predicts the wedding when Jerusalem, the center of Judah's sovereignty, is destroyed. This positively identifies the time of the fall of Jerusalem as *the last days of Israel*, and, it identifies the time of Christ coming into the kingdom as well. This means that the coming of the kingdom is not an "end of the Christian Age" theme. We confirm this by turning now to the book of Hebrews, to see the beautiful harmony in scripture concerning the last days.

HEBREWS:
THE PASSING OF THE SCEPTER FROM JUDAH

While a great deal could be said about the book of Hebrews, the passing of the scepter from Judah and the establishment of the kingdom of the Messiah, we will confine our comments to chapter 9:8-28, with referent to other supporting verses:

"The Holy Spirit is signifying this, that the way into the holy place has not yet been disclosed, while the outer tabernacle is still standing, which is a symbol for the present time. Accordingly both gifts and sacrifices are offered which cannot make the worshiper perfect in conscience, since they relate to food and drink and various washings, regulations for the body imposed until a time of reformation." (NASV)

First, note that the inspired writer tells us that the Mosaic System was supposed to end, and give way to better things. This means that the Mosaic System was supposed to have "last days." By the way, we might ask at this juncture, why the Old Covenant was supposed to pass. It was supposed to pass because it could not make anyone righteous (Galatians 3:20f). It was supposed to pass because it was based on sacrifices that could never take away sin (Hebrews 10:1-4). It was supposed to pass because it was a mere shadow of better things (Hebrews 10:1-4). It was supposed to end because it could never provide the worshiper with the clean conscience (Hebrews 9:6-10; 10:2-4).

Here is the point. The New Covenant of Jesus does provide righteousness (Romans 6:16f). The New Covenant is built on the perfect and efficacious sacrifice of Jesus (Hebrews 9:12f). The New Covenant of Jesus takes away sin (Hebrews 8:6f). If the Old Covenant World was destined to end because of its deficiencies, but the New Covenant of Christ does what the Old could not do, then why would the New Covenant Age ever come to an end? Remember, it was the Old Covenant, *nationalistic kingdom of David* that could not provide what Jesus and the New Covenant does provide. Why would God restore that ineffective Mosaic and Davidic kingdom when it could not do what God desired?[13] Thus, once again, we see the eternal nature of the New Covenant of Christ, and the temporary nature of the Old Covenant World of Israel. It was the Old Covenant Age that was supposed to end, not the New Covenant Age.

Second, notice that the Mosaic System was still standing as valid when the writer was living. Notice the present tense verbs. That is why we utilized the New American Standard text. It correctly notes that the verbs in the text are in the present tense, whereas, unfortunately, many translations do not do this.

Third, the Old Covenant World of Israel was *prophetic of the coming "time of reformation."* This means that Israel's destiny, her goal, was to be realized at "the time of reformation." Since the writer tells us that those sacrifices and practices were *temporary*, only to last until that time of reformation, it makes *no sense* to speak of a future restoration of Israel's sacrificial system. Israel's system was supposed to pass with the coming of the Messiah's kingdom. Yet, we are told by the millennialists that the Old Covenant Temple and its sacrificial system is supposed to be restored. The millennial view has turned the scriptures on their head.

The "time of reformation" is from a Greek word *diorthosis*, (*Strong's Concordance* #1357), and means to restore to a proper condition, to put something back like it is supposed to be. It was used of medical practices of healing. A sick person was healed. A broken leg was set, etc.

In Hebrews, *diorthosis* anticipated the arrival of the Messianic Kingdom, and that is the way the word is used by the Old Testament prophets. In Isaiah 62:7, the prophet anticipated the time when Jehovah would save Israel and, "make (*diorthosis*), Jerusalem a blessing." Not only did Isaiah say the anticipated *diorthosis* would come with the judgment coming of Jehovah, Hebrews says the Old Covenant System would stand until the time of the *diorthosis*, and that would be at the time of salvation (Hebrews 9:28). Could anyone doubt that the coming of *salvation* would be the time of *diorthosis*, of healing and restoration?

Fourth, the time of salvation, at the time of the *diorthosis*, is therefore placed, *not at the end of the Christian Age*, but at the end of the Old Covenant World of Israel.

Fifth, it needs to be emphasized that *nothing* exemplified the scepter of Judah more than the Old Covenant Temple with its priesthood, its sacrifices, and its worship. But, what do we have here in chapter 9? We have the prediction that the Temple, with its worship and its temple, was *temporary*, and would give way, *the scepter would depart from Judah*, when the time of the *diorthosis* came. The time of the *diorthosis* would be the time when the Messiah would bring salvation (9:28).

The scepter would pass from Judah in the last days of Israel (Genesis 49:1, 10). But the scepter passed from Judah with the destruction of Jerusalem and the Temple in A.D. 70. Therefore, the last days of Israel occurred with the destruction of Jerusalem and the Temple in A.D. 70.

Sixth, it is clear from Hebrews 9, that the "last days" are not the last days of time, or the Christian Age. The Hebrew writer says the *Old Covenant world* was, when he wrote "ready to pass away" (Hebrews 8:13). The last days climaxed with the fall of Jerusalem in A.D. 70.[14] We turn now to examine the passing of the scepter from Judah as portrayed in the book of Revelation.

THE PASSING OF THE SCEPTER FROM JUDAH, THE LAST DAYS AND REVELATION

As we have seen, the time of the coming of the kingdom belonged to the last days of Israel that consummated with the fall of Jerusalem in A.D. 70. This is confirmed in Revelation.

Now, no one would doubt that Revelation is about the ultimate last days, *no matter how you define that term.* This being true, if we can demonstrate that the Apocalypse agrees with the prediction of Genesis 49, then we have confined the definition of the last days to the consummation of God's covenant dealings with Israel.

What then do we find in Revelation? We find the golden thread of Genesis 49 running straight through the book. Take note of Revelation 5. In this chapter a sealed scroll was found in heaven. A search was made in heaven and earth for someone worthy to open the book. No one was found worthy to reveal its contents. John wept because no one could open the book. However, he was consoled in verse 5: "One of the elders said to me, 'Do not weep. Behold, the Lion of the tribe of Judah, the root of David, has prevailed to open the scroll and to loose its seven seals.'"

In one powerful verse, John brings together Genesis 49 and Isaiah 11, and lets us know that the Apocalypse is about the fulfillment of these prophecies. Revelation is surely about the fulfillment of Isaiah's prediction of the New Creation, for in chapter 21-22, John alludes directly to Isaiah 65, and tells us that he was anticipating the fulfillment of the prophets.

We need to see several things about Revelation as it relates to Genesis 49 and the last days.

First, Revelation is about the establishment of the kingdom of Messiah, the Lion of Judah. In Revelation 11, at the time of judgment– *and isn't that a "last days" concept?*– "the kingdoms of this world have become the kingdoms of our Lord and of His Christ." (v. 15). In other words, at the time of the judgment, Shiloh would receive his kingdom. Genesis 49 would be fulfilled at the time of the judgment. But Genesis 49 is about the last days of Israel, not the last days of the Christian Age.

Second, *the time of the judgment is the time of the judgment of Judah.* How do we know this? Because the judgment scene in Revelation 11 is the time of the judgment of the city, *"where the Lord was slain" (Revelation 11:8).* Is there any doubt about where Jesus was crucified? He was not slain in the Roman Catholic Church. He was not slain in ancient, or restored, Babylon. He was not slain in New York City. Thus, in Revelation, Shiloh would receive his kingdom when Jerusalem, the capital of Judah, and the symbol of Judah's sovereignty, was destroyed.

Third, Revelation is not about the restoration of national Judah. Biblically the "restoration of Israel" that people talk about so much, was to occur in the spiritual body of Christ, which is exactly what we see in Revelation 7 and 14.[15] The establishment of the kingdom of "the Lion of tribe Judah" would necessitate the removal of the scepter from Judah, just as Genesis 49 predicted.

Fourth, when the city that killed the Lord falls, in chapter 18-19, at the coming of Shiloh, the New Creation predicted by Isaiah 11, and 65 becomes a reality.

Now, here is something that is fascinating, and it demonstrates the unity of scripture in a marvelous way. Isaiah 65 predicted that Israel would fill up the measure of her sin and be destroyed. A new people in the New Creation would follow. The kingdom would be taken from Judah and given to a new people.[16]

In Revelation, Babylon fills up the measure of her sin, is destroyed, and the New Creation foretold by Isaiah arrives. Thus, at the fall of the city guilty of killing God's prophets, the kingdom passes to the Messiah.

What is so fascinating about this is that, as we have seen, everyone admits that in Revelation we are dealing with last days ideas. Well, watch carefully. Isaiah said that the New Creation would come when Israel had filled the measure of her sin and was destroyed. The kingdom of Messiah would be established as the New Creation.

Jesus, in Matthew 23, and Paul, in 1 Thessalonians 2:15f, said that Israel was going to fill up the measure of her sin, by persecuting the saints, and be destroyed in that first century generation.

John, in Revelation depicts the city where the Lord was slain as filling up the measure of her sin, being destroyed, and the New Creation following. Not only that, he said the prophecy was "at hand" and, "must shortly come to pass." (Revelation 1:1-3).

By confining the fulfillment of the prophecy of filling up the measure of sin and being destroyed *to his generation*, Jesus identified the focus of the last days as the last days of Israel, and, even more, he confined the consummation of the last days to his generation: "Verily I say unto you, all these things shall come upon this generation" (Matthew 23:36). Once again, we see that the last days have nothing to do with the last days of time, or the last days of the Christian Age.

In Revelation, we have the transference of sovereignty from one city to another. A city called Babylon dressed in purple and royal attire, is destroyed, and the new Jerusalem stands triumphant as the city of God. Just as Jesus said, "The kingdom shall be taken from you and given to another nation," Revelation depicts the loss of sovereignty by one city, and the transference of that sovereignty to another entity, *the city of Shiloh*!

> **Revelation is about the fulfillment of Genesis 49. But Genesis 49 is about the last days of Israel, (not the last days of time or the Christian Age). Therefore, Revelation is about the last days of Israel!**

Thus, from Genesis to Revelation, the theme of the transference of sovereignty from Judah to Messiah is a consistent theme. And we must emphasize that Jacob placed these events in the last days of Israel/Judah, not in the last days of the Christian Age. Since Revelation is without doubt about the events of "the last days," and it is equally without doubt about the fulfillment of *the prophecy of Genesis 49, it is patently clear that Revelation is not about the end of the Christian Age, nor about the end of time. Revelation is about the last days of Israel that consummated with the destruction of Jerusalem in A.D. 70.* As Holford wrote, in that event: "The Jewish state indeed, at this time, was fitly compared to a carcass. The scepter of Judah–i.e. its civil and political authority, the life of its religion and the glory of the temple–was departed.[17]

Let us turn now to an Old Testament passage that is considered to be a key last days text by our dispensational friends.

DEUTERONOMY 4:30-31
"When you are in distress and all these things come upon you in the latter days, when you turn to the Lord your God and obey His voice (for the Lord your God is a merciful God) He will not forsake you nor destroy you, nor forget the covenant of your fathers which He swore to them."

In his written debate with Kenneth Gentry, Ice said that this passage, and the book of Deuteronomy as a whole, "provides a prophetic roadmap of Israel's history."[18]

Before we examine this passage in detail, we need to point out that it is actually a total refutation of a vitally important millennial doctrine. In the glossy book *Charting the End Times*, LaHaye and Ice insist that the "restoration" of Israel that occurred in 1948 is a "Super Sign of the End Times." The problem of 1948 is that even as their book acknowledges, the majority of Jews that returned to the land were *atheists and skeptics*! To solve that problem, LaHaye and Ice claim that God actually foretold a re-gathering of Israel *in unbelief.* See my book *Israel:1948, Countdown to No Where,* for a total refutation of that claim.[19] For the moment however, we want to notice some things from the text before us.

First, if Deuteronomy 4, is a, "prophetic road map of Israel's history," *it completely omits* any mention of a re-gathering, at any time, in *unbelief.* In fact, in verse 30 the condition for God's blessing is repentance and obedience. Thus, in a key "last days" passage there is no provision for what Ice and LaHaye call the "Super Sign of the End Times," Israel's return to the land in unbelief. This is a major problem to say the least. Wouldn't you think that if Deuteronomy 4 was the prophetic road map for Israel's last days that it should include the pivotal re-gathering in unbelief? If a re-gathering in unbelief is *the key last days sign*, shouldn't it be included in this key last days text? The complete omission of a return in unbelief, and the emphasis on *repentance* for a return from captivity, belies the millennial application of Deuteronomy 4 to the events of 1948.

Second, if the passage deals with Israel's yet future condition, then it clearly predicts that Israel will one day go into *idolatry again*, and be scattered into captivity for that sin *again*. Notice verses 25 and 28. Moses said that when Israel was in the land, *and began to worship other gods*, that Jehovah would then scatter them to other lands, in captivity, and there they would worship other gods also. Do the millennialists believe this will happen at some point in the future? No. Do they believe that Israel was guilty of idolatry in 1948? No.

Even the millennialists insist that the Babylonian captivity cured Israel of her idolatrous ways. *Charting*, (p. 105) says, "Israel seemed to get the message, (of punishment for idolatry, DKP) for the (Babylonian, DKP) captivity cured them from ever again worshiping idols as a nation." Merrill Unger said: "The Babylonian captivity cured Israel of idolatry"[20] Well, if the Babylonian Captivity cured Israel of idolatry, then the situation of Deuteronomy 4:25, 30 hardly applies to a yet future situation, or to the situation of 1948.

Third, and this is *major*, the Mosaic Covenant, which of course includes Deuteronomy 4, *is no longer valid*. This is where the rub comes in for the millennial view. The Mosaic Covenant, even according to Ice, "has forever been fulfilled and discontinued through Christ." (*Prophecy*, 258) Our point is, that if the Mosaic Covenant–inclusive of Deuteronomy 4–has been *removed forever*, then you cannot appeal to Deuteronomy 4 as a road map for yet future events concerning Israel! The only way for Deuteronomy 4, or Deuteronomy 30, to be applied to the future, is for the Mosaic Covenant to be *restored*. Do the millennialists believe that the Mosaic Covenant will be restored? No. This is an inescapable problem.

So, to recap, we have this situation.

> **If the Mosaic Covenant has been forever removed, then the millennialists cannot appeal to the Mosaic Covenant for predictions of modern day events.**
> **If the Mosaic Covenant is gone, then its promises are *fulfilled*!**

1.) The millennialists claim that Deuteronomy 4:30f, is a key prophetic roadmap of Israel's history.

2.) But the millennialists also teach that the Mosaic Covenant–which is inclusive of Deuteronomy 4--has been *forever* removed.

3.) The millennialists do not believe that the Mosaic Covenant will be restored.

4.) Yet, the millennialists appeal to Deuteronomy 4 to prove that the events of 1948, and events like the Great Tribulation, are the fulfillment of that text, and/or are yet future.

How in the name of reason can you appeal to a nullified covenant as the basis for yet future events? If that Covenant is removed then all of its provisions are *null and void*. It is fundamentally illogical for the millennialists to say that the Mosaic Covenant has been forever removed, and then appeal to the Mosaic Covenant as a roadmap for the future.

Thus, one of the "last days" texts so important to the futurist view is shown to actually refute the modern day application.

It is my position that Deuteronomy 4 is not an eschatological passage dealing with the end of the age. It is one of the rare texts in which the term "last days" simply means "at a later time." As you read Israel's history the outline of events found in Deuteronomy 4 occur repeatedly. That is, Israel sinned. God punished her. She repented, and cried for relief, and God delivered her. See the book of Judges as an excellent example of the out-playing of the Deuteronomic pattern. And, since the pattern of Deuteronomy 4 was played out in the events of the book of Judges, it can hardly be argued that the book of Judges records events of the "last days!"

Deuteronomy 4 cannot be applied to future events without demanding a restoration of the Mosaic Covenant. Yet God has removed that covenant in Christ. Thus, this passage has no application to our future. We turn now to a text that definitely did deal with Israel's last days, however, and with the end of the age.

DEUTERONOMY 32

This great chapter is called the *Song of Moses*. It is one of the most significant, yet overlooked prophecies in the Bible. I am currently working on a book about the Song to demonstrate how this prophecy is interwoven into the very fabric of the New Testament, and specifically, of Biblical eschatology. For the time being, we can focus only on a few salient points from this great prophecy to help us identify the last days.

First, the prophecy has to do with *the last days of Israel*, not the last days of time. Moses called on Israel to consider, "what their end will be...that they would consider their latter end" (Deuteronomy 32:20; 29).

Second, Moses said that in Israel's last days, she would, "become utterly corrupt and turn aside from the way which I have commanded you, and evil shall befall you in the latter days" (Deuteronomy 31:29). Since Deuteronomy 31:29 serves as the introduction to the Song of Moses, we are including our examination of it in our comments on chapter 32.

Third, in the last days, Jehovah would bring in the Gentiles in order to provoke Israel to jealousy (v. 21f).

Fourth, God said that in the last days, "The Lord shall judge His people" (v. 36). He would judge Israel because, "Her vine is the vine of Sodom" (v. 32).

Fifth, as a result of Israel's sin, the Lord said, "A fire is kindled in My anger, and shall burn to the lowest hell, it shall consume the earth with her increase, and set on fire the foundations of the mountains." (v. 22).

Sixth, in the last days, El Shaddai would, "Avenge the blood of His servants and render vengeance to His adversaries" (v. 43).

There are many other issues we could explore from this chapter, but for brevity, we will confine our comments to these issues. Let us begin by taking special note, again, that the focus of the prophecy was the last days of Israel. To interject the consummation of the Christian Aeon, or the end of time into the chapter is without merit. Thus, just like Genesis 49, the Biblical focus and identity of the last days is the last days of Israel. It is time for the modern church to bring its teaching in line with scripture!

Moses said that in the last days, Israel would become *utterly corrupt*, and evil would befall her. Here, we are on absolutely safe ground in identifying the framework and time of the last days.

In Acts 7:52, Stephen stood in the Temple and castigated the Jews for their long, bloody history of killing the prophets: "Which of the prophets have you not slain?" Jesus had earlier said that they would, by killing the apostles and prophets he was going to send, fill up the measure of their sin. They were going to become *utterly corrupt*, just like Moses predicted they would "in the last days." (Deuteronomy 31:29) Finally, Jesus said judgment for that full cup of sin would be poured out in his generation (v. 34-36). Remember the parable of Matthew 21 and the wicked husbandmen. They exhausted the patience of the master by killing the servants sent to them. The harmony with Deuteronomy is direct.

Thus, Moses said that in the last days, Israel would become utterly corrupt, fill the measure of her sin, and be judged. Jesus, who appeared in the last days (Hebrews 1:1), said Israel would fill the cup of her sin and be judged in her generation. It is clear that Jesus was not speaking to or about the church. He was not speaking about any so-called end of time. He was speaking of what was going to happen *to Israel*, in his generation. This means, unequivocally, that the *last days* foretold by Deuteronomy 32 would be in existence during Jesus' generation, but would come to consummation when she was judged. And, it should go without saying that the judgment Jesus was referring to was the judgment that fell on Jerusalem in A.D. 70.

The third point, we covered #s 1 and 2 together, is that Moses said that in the last days, Jehovah would call the Gentiles to Him in order to make Israel jealous. Remember now, that Moses was speaking of *Israel's* last days in Deuteronomy 32. Not the last days of time or the church. And, he said that in Israel's last days God would call the Gentiles. (God was not promising to call the Gentiles in order to make the *church* jealous).

This means that the last days of Israel could not have been suspended due to the rejection of Jesus by the Jews. Now, our premillennial friends insist that Jesus came to establish the kingdom, but due to the Jewish rejection of Jesus, the kingdom was postponed: "At His first advent, the Lord Jesus Christ came to offer the Kingdom promised in the Old Testament. When Israel rejected her Messiah, the Old Testament program was held in abeyance."[21] According to the millennialists, the 70th week of Daniel 9, and the famous 70 weeks prediction, was suspended, and Israel's last days were put on hold until the Rapture. The 69th week supposedly ended when Jesus rode into Jerusalem, being hailed as king. Thus, from that point forward, Israel's last days are in abeyance until the Rapture. But here is the problem.

Moses said that in Israel's last days, Jehovah would call the Gentiles to Him. However, the Gentiles were not called to Jehovah by the preaching of the Gospel until some 10 years after the day of Pentecost. The conversion of Cornelius (Acts 10), signaled the ministry to the Gentiles, and then, the conversion of Paul began the Gentile mission in earnest.

As a matter of fact, Paul was the special apostle to call the Gentiles, and, here is what is so important, he specifically quotes from Deuteronomy 32 to justify his ministry to the Gentiles (Romans 10:19). In other words, Paul saw his ministry to the Gentiles as the fulfillment of the Song of

Moses. But if Paul's ministry was the fulfillment of the Song of Moses, this means that the last days of Israel were in existence during Paul's ministry, long after the so-called suspension of the last days of Israel. This is absolutely devastating to the premillennial view!

If the last days foretold by Moses, in Deuteronomy 32, were in existence during Paul's ministry,[22] then undeniably, the countdown of Israel's last days was not suspended as our premillennial friends say. If the countdown of Israel's last days was on-going during Paul's ministry, then since Jesus placed the consummation of those last days at the fall of Jerusalem, as we have just seen, this means that the last days of Israel cannot in any way be placed in the future.

> **Deuteronomy said that in Israel's last days the Gentiles would be called. Paul said his ministry to the Gentiles was the fulfillment of Deuteronomy 32, and that the end of the age had arrived. This can only mean that the last days of Israel existed during Paul's ministry. But if this is so, millennialism is wrong!**

Further, since Paul's ministry to the Gentiles was the fulfillment of Deuteronomy 32, this means that the last days foretold by that prophecy was the focus of his ministry as well. This means that when Paul said, "the time has been shortened" (1 Corinthians 7:26f), and, "the end of the ages has come upon us" (1 Corinthians 10:11), that we need to see these statements in the context of *Israel's last days*. After all, isn't it pretty clear that Paul was *not* saying, "The end of the Christian Age has drawn near"? If he was, he was patently wrong, and, if he was wrong, Christianity falls.

It cannot be over-emphasized that the focus of Deuteronomy 32 is on *the last days of Israel*. To apply that prophecy to the last days of the current age is wrong. Yet, most commentators, when speaking of the conversion of the Gentiles in Romans, focus on the Christian Age, and its supposed end at the *parousia* (coming) of Christ. This is anachronistic. It removes Paul's discussion far beyond the temporal and covenantal parameters of Deuteronomy and the other Old Testament prophecies he cites. Paul was focused on the fulfillment of God's promises to Israel, not the end of the Christian Age.

Moses said that in the last days, "The Lord shall judge His people," and the reason for that is, "Their vine is the vine of Sodom" (Deuteronomy 32:32, 36). A great deal could be said about these two verses from Deuteronomy. We will only note a few things.

Paul, in Romans 12:19, comforted the Christians being persecuted, by quoting from Deuteronomy 32:35. In Hebrews 10:30, in the identical context of persecution, he quotes the same verses. Now, it is important to see that the persecution against the church in the first century was primarily instigated by the Jews. So, in both Romans and Hebrews, Christians were being persecuted by the Jews. Paul promised the Christians relief from that persecution by quoting the promise of Moses that in Israel's last days, they would be judged. Paul was applying the last days prophecy of the judgment of Israel to *his contemporary generation*, and applying that prophecy to the Jews of his day who were persecuting the True Israel of God.

In Hebrews 10 the impending judgment on the persecutors, and the attendant salvation for the faithful, was coming, "in a very, very little while" (Greek, *hosan, hosan micron*). (Hebrews 10:37). Since the judgment foretold by Deuteronomy, the judgment being promised by Hebrews, was to be in the last days, and the Hebrew writer said it was very, very near, the writer clearly believed he was living in Israel's last days. So, once again, the focus of the last days is not the Christian Age.

The fourth point is that Moses said Israel was to be judged because her vine was, "the vine of Sodom" (Deuteronomy 32:32). This brings us again to see the beautiful harmony in the Bible. In Revelation, we find the judgment of the harlot city. Remember, this is, "where the Lord was slain" (Revelation 11:8). But did you notice that this harlot city was also, "spiritually called Sodom"? So, Revelation, which is about the fulfillment of God's promise concerning Judah and Shiloh, is also about the judgment of Jerusalem, whom He calls *Sodom*. The prophecy of Moses was being fulfilled in her.

Here is something amazing. The only city, in all the Bible, that is ever spiritually called Sodom was *Old Covenant Jerusalem*! As a matter of fact, the only city, other than historical Sodom, to *ever* be called Sodom at all, was *Jerusalem!*[23] See Isaiah 1:9-10, Jeremiah 23:14 and Ezekiel 16:35-49. So, here is what we have. Moses said that in the last days, Israel would bear the fruit of being the vine of Sodom. John, writing about the last days, says, "Babylon"–the city where the Lord was slain– was spiritually called Sodom, and was about to be destroyed. John had the fulfillment of Deuteronomy 32 in mind. By the way, he refers to the Song of Moses more than once in the Apocalypse, so, like Paul, John was concerned with the fulfillment of that prophecy of Israel's last days.

The fifth point above is that in Israel's last days, Jehovah would be so angry at that nation that He would *burn up the earth* (Deuteronomy 32:22). Here is an interesting question: Does *anyone* teach that at the so-called end of time, or at the end of the Christian Age, the literal earth is burned up *because God is angry with Israel?* Answer: No. I am unaware of any school of eschatology that teaches that at some point in the future, God will be so angry at Israel that He will destroy the literal cosmos.

What does this mean then? This is metaphoric language. It means that in Israel's last days, Jehovah would destroy Israel, her Temple, her world. God would destroy Israel's "heaven and earth." He would destroy her *covenant* world.[24] Unless you are willing to posit a future destruction of Israel at the end of the Christian Age, or at the end of the millennium, then you must take the language metaphorically. The beauty of this is that we have Jesus' words that in his generation, Israel's "heaven and earth" was indeed going to be destroyed, *at his coming in judgment of Jerusalem* (Matthew 24:29-34). Thus, Moses said that in Israel's last days, Israel's sin would lead to the destruction of "creation." Jesus, who appeared in the last days, predicted the destruction of Israel's "heaven and earth." The harmony of scripture is evident, and the identification of the last days is confined to a referent to the last days of Israel.

The sixth and final point we want to make from Deuteronomy 32 is that Jehovah said that in the last days, He would, "Avenge the blood of His servants" (v. 43). This is an important promise, and one developed throughout scriptures. In my book, *Like Father, Like Son: Coming on Clouds of Glory*, I develop at length the Biblical theme of the vindication of the martyrs, the Law of Blood Atonement, Filling the Measure of Sin and Suffering, and similar motifs. We cannot develop these motifs and themes here, but refer you to that work.[25]

What did Adonay mean by the promise to vindicate the blood of His saints? It is referent to the fact that historically, He had sent His prophets to Israel, repeatedly, to call them to repentance and holiness. In response, Israel had repeatedly rejected and killed the prophets. Nehemiah recounted Israel's history: "They were disobedient and rebelled against You, Cast Your law behind their backs and killed Your prophets who testified against them" (Nehemiah 9:26; see 1 Kings 18:4).

Repeatedly, the Lord accused Israel of having hands red with the blood of His saints (see Isaiah 1:15; Isaiah 59, 3, 6, 7; Jeremiah 2, 22:17; Ezekiel 22, etc.) Israel was judged in B. C. 721, and Judah was judged in B. C. 586 for killing the righteous. However, Deuteronomy 32 looked to the last days and the "final" judgment for killing the Lord's servants.

Remember what Jesus said in Matthew 23? We have shown how Jesus, who appeared on the last days, stood in the temple, and recounted Israel's history of killing the righteous, "O Jerusalem, Jerusalem, thou that killest the prophets, and stones them that are sent unto her!"

In one of his most famous of parables, that of the Importunate Widow (Luke 18), Jesus spoke of the righteous, suffering at the hands of their persecutors. He said the martyrs, "Cry out to Him (God, DKP) day and night." Their cry was for *vindication*, the identical word used in Deuteronomy 32:43, in God's promise to *vindicate* the blood of His martyrs in the last days. This is also the word used in Revelation 6:9-11, where we see the martyrs under the altar crying, "How long, O Lord, will you not *avenge* us on those who dwell on the earth?" (Revelation 6:9-11).

Moses said that in the last days God would avenge the shed blood of His saints. Jesus said that all the blood of all the martyrs, all the way back to creation, would be avenged in his generation, in the fall of Jerusalem. The last days foretold by Moses therefore climax in the fall of Jerusalem in A.D. 70.

The stream of the martyrs blood flows throughout scriptures, and it flows through the street of one city, Old Covenant Jerusalem. From Deuteronomy 32 through Revelation the stream flows, yet, in Deuteronomy 32, Jehovah promised that *in the last days*, He would finally avenge that shed blood. So, when was that promise to be fulfilled? Was it to be at the end of the Christian Age, or at the end of time? Not if we are willing to accept the inspired words of the Son of God. Read Matthew 23:33-34:

"Serpents, brood of vipers! How can you escape the condemnation of hell? Therefore, indeed I send you prophets, wise men and scribes; some of them you will kill and crucify, and some of them you will scourge in your synagogues and persecute from city to city, that on you may come all the righteous blood shed on the earth, from the blood of righteous Abel to the blood of Zechariah, the son of Berechiah, whom you murdered between the temple and the altar. Assuredly I say to you, all these things shall come upon this generation." (Matthew 23:33-36).

If we are going to accept Jesus as Lord, and his word as authoritative, we must bow before his statement that the vindication of the martyrs was to occur *in his generation at the fall of Jerusalem*. And, this helps us positively identify and delimit the last days.

Moses said that *in the last days*, i.e. Israel's last days, God would avenge the shed blood of His saints (Deuteronomy 32:43).

But Jesus, who appeared in the last days (Hebrews 1:1-2), said all the blood of the martyrs, all the way back to creation, would be avenged in the fall of Jerusalem in A.D. 70.

Therefore, the last days foretold by Moses, the last days of Israel, occurred in the fall of Jerusalem in A.D. 70.

We must emphasize how destructive this is to the millennial view. Remember that the millennial view is that the last days of Israel were suspended when Jesus was rejected in Matthew 12, and that the 69th week of Daniel 9 ended with the triumphant entry into Jerusalem in Matthew 21. Jack Van Impe says that when Jesus died, "At that very moment, the prophetic clock stopped as far as Daniel's vision is concerned and 70 years later the Jews were dispossessed of their country and scattered throughout the world."[26] The consummative last days of Israel will begin with the signing of the peace treaty by the Anti-Christ and Israel following the Rapture, according to this view, and could not have been present in A.D. 70. If the last days of Israel were present in A.D. 70, the entire premillennial view is destroyed!

This is not an overstatement for dramatic effect. Ice, a leading dispensationalist, says in a series of articles on Daniel 9, that if there is no gap, of so far 2000 years, between the 69th and 70th week of Daniel, then, "the dispensational system falls apart."[27]

With this in mind, look again our argument. Moses said the blood of the martyrs would be avenged *in the last days of Israel.* Jesus said the blood of the martyrs would be avenged in the fall of Jerusalem *in AD 70.*[28] Therefore, the last days of Israel existed in A.D. 70. There is no escape from this argument. Israel's last days existed in A.D. 70. Therefore, "the Dispensational system falls apart."

The Biblical *fact*, of the time of the vindication of the blood of the martyrs, is equally destructive to the traditional Amillennial and Postmillennial definition of the last days. Here is why.

The Amillennial and Postmillennial view is that the martyrs are vindicated at the end of the Christian Age. Years ago, I listened to a sermon on the last days by a college professor friend of mine, an Amillennialist. He quoted Matthew 23:34-35, and said, "one of these days," at the end of the Christian Age, all the martyrs will be vindicated. The problem is that this is *not* what Matthew 23 says.

Here is why this is so important. The Amillennialists and Postmillennialists say that the true last days belong to the end of the Christian Age. However, the Bible affirms, as shown above, that *the Christian Age has no end.* The point is that the Bible undeniably places the time of the vindication of the martyrs in the last days. However, the Bible is equally emphatic that the martyrs were to be vindicated at the destruction of Jerusalem in A.D. 70. This means that if the time of the vindication of the martyrs is indeed at the end of the Christian Age, then the Christian Age ended in AD 70 (which, of course, is ludicrous), or the amillennial and postmillennial views are wrong. I choose the latter.

The issue is actually simple. Moses and Jesus said the vindication of the martyrs would occur *in Israel's last days*. The amillennial and Postmillennialists say that the vindication of the martyrs will occur *in the last days of the Christian Age*. Who shall we believe? I choose to accept the words of Moses, Jesus, and the New Testament writers. The vindication of the martyrs was to occur *in the last days of Israel*. This is supported by John in the Apocalypse.

Remember, in Revelation 6, we saw the martyrs crying for vindication. They were then given white robes and told to, "rest for a little while, until their fellow-brethren who should suffer as they did, should be filled." The next seal vision was of their vindication at the Day of the Lord. Let's make this short and simple.

The vindication of the martyrs would occur with the fall of "Babylon" (Revelation 11:8-17; 18:20-24).

But "Babylon" of Revelation was Old Covenant Jerusalem (Revelation 11:8).

Conclusion: Therefore, the vindication of the martyrs would occur with the fall of Old Covenant Jerusalem.

As a corollary argument to help us confirm our identification of the last days consider the following.

The vindication of the martyrs was to occur in the last days of Israel (Deuteronomy 32:43).

But the vindication of the martyrs was to occur with the fall of Jerusalem in AD 70 (Matthew 23).

Conclusion: Therefore, the last days of Israel occurred in A.D. 70.

Remember now, everyone agrees that Revelation is about the "real" last days, not a preliminary last days. The last days of Revelation are the *true* last days to wrap up God's Scheme of Redemption. Thus, to identify the last days in Revelation is to identify the last days of all of eschatological focus. We have shown that the last days of Revelation are the last days of Israel that ended in A.D. 70. Therefore, the last days that are the focus of Biblical eschatology are the last days of Israel, not the last days of the Christian Age.

Genesis 49 and Deuteronomy 32 are in perfect agreement. These two passages form the foundation of much of the Biblical teachings about the kingdom and the last days. Yet, as we have seen, neither of these passages is concerned with the end of the Church Age. The same is true of the third major text we will examine.

ISAIAH 2-4

When Bible students discuss the last days prophecies of the kingdom, Isaiah 2-4 is one of the first passages cited, especially verses 2f of chapter 2. However, to omit a study of chapters 3-4 is to do a great disservice to proper exegesis. We cannot do an exhaustive analysis of these chapters but we do need to note some vital facts.

First, it says that in the last days, that is, *while the days would be in existence*, the kingdom would be established. It *does not say* that the establishment of the kingdom would bring in the last days. It *does not say* the last days would be established when the kingdom was established. It says, "In the last days, the mountain of the house of the Lord will be established." *The last days would already be in existence when the kingdom would be established.* This means, unequivocally that the establishment of the church on Pentecost occurred in the midst of *the already present* last days. This is critical.

Second, the last days foretold by Isaiah would consummate when Jehovah would judge Israel. (See chapter 2:9-11; 19-21). What is so important here is that Jesus, in Luke 23:28f, directly alludes to these verses in a context that is an undisputed reference and prediction of the judgment of Jerusalem in A.D. 70. In other words, Isaiah predicted the time when men would run to the hills for protection. (Does it not go without saying that it would do no good to run *anywhere*, if he was predicting an event that would be over, "in a moment, in the twinkling of an eye"?) Jesus, in predicting the judgment of Jerusalem cites Isaiah 2. Therefore, Isaiah's prediction of the last days judgment of Jehovah refers to the last days of Israel when Jehovah would judge Israel.

Third, this is confirmed in chapter three. You will need to take note of the "in that day" references that run all the way through chapters three and four, in order to appreciate and confirm what we are saying here, and this is vitally important. The "in that day" references refer to the close of the last days mentioned in chapter 2: "The Lord of Hosts takes away from Jerusalem and from Judah the stock and the store, the whole supply of bread." In other words, the last days would be a time of famine!

Fourth, the reason for this last days judgment is stated in chapter 3:8, "For Jerusalem stumbled, and Judah is fallen, because their tongue, and their doings are against the Lord, to provoke the eyes of His glory."

Here is a challenging question: Are there any futuristic views of the last days that teach that God is going to judge the literal earth *because of the sins of Israel?* So far as I know, there are no such last days views. Thus, we have a prediction of what was to come *on Jerusalem and Judah* in the last days. It was going to come *because of the sins of Jerusalem and Judah.* Unless your view of the last days provides for the judgment of Jerusalem and Judah as the focus, *and the reason* for the judgment, then it is out of step with scripture. Isaiah is not a prediction of the last days of the church, or the last days of the Christian Age.

Fifth, this assessment is confirmed further in 3:13f, where we are told more of this last days time of judgment. The prophet says it would be when, "The Lord stands to plead, and stands to judge the people. The Lord will enter into judgment with the elders of the people and His princes: For you have eaten up the vineyard, the plunder of the poor is in your houses."

This passage is a clear echo of Deuteronomy 32, where, if you will remember, Jehovah said that in the last days, He would judge *Israel* for her sin. Now, if Isaiah 2-4 is a reiteration of God's promise in Deuteronomy 32, then it is clear that the topic is not the last days of time, but the last days of Israel's national existence.

Sixth, the passage emphatically says that the events would be *in time events*, not *end of time* events. It says, "Your men (the men of Israel!), shall fall by the sword and your mighty men in the war" (3:25). Interestingly, Jesus alludes directly to Isaiah in a passage that virtually everyone agrees refers to the judgment of Israel in A.D. 70.

In Luke 21:24, Jesus foretold the destruction of Jerusalem, "They shall fall by the edge of the sword, and be led captive of all nations." Thus, just as Jesus alluded directly to Isaiah 2:9-11f in his prediction of the judgment of Jerusalem (Luke 23:28-31), once again, *he draws from that same prophecy* to speak of the judgment of Israel.

Seventh, Isaiah says that the Day of the Lord would be, "When the Lord has washed away the filth of the daughters of Jerusalem, and purged the blood of Jerusalem from her midst, by the spirit of judgment and the spirit of fire" (4:4). This helps greatly in identifying the last days, and the Day of the Lord.

Isaiah is predicting the events of the last days. He predicted that in the last days, *Jehovah would judge Israel for her blood guilt!* Do we have any clues as to when this would be? Yes.

In Matthew 23, Jesus stood in the Temple and rehearsed Israel's bloody history of killing the prophets, and God's righteous ones: "You are witnesses against yourselves that you are the sons of those who murdered the prophets" (23:31). He said that Israel would fill up the measure of her sin by persecuting the prophets, apostles and scribes that he was sending to her (23:32, 34). That judgment was coming on Israel, "That upon you may come all the righteous blood shed on the earth," and, it was coming in his generation, "Assuredly I say to you, all these things shall come on this generation" (v. 36).

So what do we have? The prophecy of Isaiah that said that in the last days, Israel would be judged for her bloodguilt. Jesus appeared in the last days (Hebrews 1:1-2), and at the end of the age (Hebrews 9:26), and said that Israel was going to be judged in his generation for her bloodguilt. There is a perfect agreement between Isaiah and Matthew 23. This means that the last days foretold by Isaiah are the last days of Israel, not the last days of the Church Age, or of time. It also means that the last days were consummated by the judgment of Israel in A.D. 70, since Isaiah's prediction of the last days ends with the coming of the Day of the Lord in judgment of Israel.

In the normal flow of our study, we would examine the prophecies of Daniel at this juncture. However, since Daniel's prophecies play such a pivotal role in identifying the last days, we will reserve our examination of that book until a bit later. So, for now, we turn to the book of Hosea.

HOSEA 3:4F

"The children of Israel shall abide many days without a king or prince, without a sacrifice or sacred pillar, without an ephod or teraphim. Afterward the children of Israel shall return and seek the Lord their God and David their king. They shall fear the Lord and His goodness in the latter days." (Hosea 3:4-5).

There are several things to be gleaned from this text.

First, this prediction, like the others we have examined so far, concerns the last days of *Israel*. The prophecy is not about the end of time, or the last days of the church. It really is quite amazing, from what we have seen so far, that anyone would even remotely associate the "last days" with the end of time, or the end of the Christian Age, for there is not one thing in any of the texts we have, or will, examine to suggest such an idea.

Second, Jehovah was about to remove the king of Israel from the throne by taking the nation into captivity (Hosea 13:9f).

Third, Israel would be without a king until the last days (v. 5).

Fourth, in the last days, Israel would serve "David" their king. This is a prediction of Jesus, the son of David, not David personally.

Fifth, in the last days, when Israel served her King, she would be restored, and married once again to Him (Hosea 2:19). The rejection she had suffered when He had divorced her would be put aside, and, "In the place where it was said of them, 'You are not my people There it shall be said of them, 'You are the sons of the living God...I will have mercy on her who had not obtained mercy; Then I will say to those who were not my people, You are my people.'" (Hosea 1:10; 2:23).

Sixth, from these facts it is evident that the last days were not present in Hosea's day. The last days were far off, since Israel would exist for *a long time* until the last days came (v. 4). By the way, that "long time" period was from B. C. 721 to the time of Jesus. Those who claim that time statements in scripture don't really mean what they say must explain why the time statement here is so prosaic, *and clearly did mean a long time*, in the way that man views time.

Okay, now, let's take a look at the elements of Hosea's prediction in the light of what the New Testament had to say.

First, the writers affirmed that they were living in the last days foretold by the prophets of Israel (Acts 2:15f; 3:19f). More on this below.

Second, Peter said that Jesus, the son of David had been raised up into heaven to sit on David's throne. He had been made, "both Lord and Christ" in fulfillment of the promises made to David. (Acts 2:29-36). Thus, when Israel obeyed the apostles on Pentecost, they were serving "David."

Third, and this is *critical*, in his epistle, Peter said he was living in the last days (1 Peter 1:20), foretold by the Old Testament prophets (1 Peter 1:10). It must be remembered that according to the millennialists, *the Old Testament writers never even mentioned the Church Age*. They spoke and wrote only of the last days of Israel, and what would happen then. Well, Peter said that the events happening in his day were the events foretold by the Old Testament prophets, and that he was living in the last times. This means, without any question, that Peter was living in the last days of Israel.

However, if Peter, writing in A.D. 63-65 was living in the last days of Israel, foretold by the Old Testament prophets, then the millennial view that Israel's last days were postponed during the personal ministry of Jesus is categorically proven to be wrong.

Fourth, not only did Peter say that he was living in the last days foretold by the Old Testament prophets, he informs us that he is writing about the fulfillment of the Old Testament prophecies of the salvation of Israel. Take a look at point #5 above, from Hosea. That prophet said that in the last days, Israel, once cast off, and assimilated into the Gentiles to such a degree that she was no longer considered the people of God, would once again be restored to her God:

> "In the place where it was said of them, 'You are not my people,' There it shall be said of them, 'You are the sons of the living God...I will have mercy on her who had not obtained mercy; Then I will say to those who were not my people, You are my people!'" (Hosea 1:10; 2:23).

In 1 Peter 2:9f, the inspired apostle *directly quotes* this promise to speak of the church as the fulfillment of Hosea's prediction. What is the point? The point is that Peter was *the apostle to the circumcision*, that is, to Israel. And, in 1 Peter, this apostle quotes one of the most significant last days promises made to and about Israel. It is the promise of the time when Jehovah would save Israel, under her Messiah, after she had apostatized, but then returned. Peter was addressing Christians, *(members of the 10 Tribes of the Diaspora, who had become members of the body of Christ)*, and tells them that they had become what Hosea predicted:

> "You are a chosen generation, a royal priesthood, a holy nation,[29] His own special people, that you may proclaim the praises of Him who called you out of darkness into His marvelous light, who once were not a people but are now the people of God, who had not obtained mercy but now have obtained mercy."

Notice that Peter was addressing his epistle to "The pilgrims of the *dispersion*" (1 Peter 1:1), the word *diaspora* is the technical term for Israel - the ten tribes - scattered among the Gentiles. There could hardly be a clearer affirmation that the Old Testament prophecies, including Hosea, were being fulfilled. Peter said that the recipients of his epistle were the fulfillment of Hosea's prophecy. He said, "You are!" He did not say, "I am using Hosea's promise to prove that Israel will one day be restored." He said to those Christians, "You are!," and no amount of denial can make his words mean, "You are *not*!" Yet, Hosea's prophecy was about what would happen in *Israel's last days*. Therefore, Peter was living in Israel's last days.

Fifth, consider what Hosea said about the *wedding*. He said that in the last days, God would once again marry Israel[30] (Hosea 2:19f). It is important to remember that Jesus came to confirm the promises made to Israel (Romans 15:8), and that one of his favorite themes was the Wedding Feast (Matthew 22; Luke 14) And, Jesus repeatedly said the time was near.

Paul the apostle likewise spoke about the wedding, and it must be remembered that Paul only preached "the hope of Israel" (Acts 24, 26, 28). Yet, while Paul preached the hope of Israel, he spoke of the wedding between Christ and the *Church* (Ephesians 5:25f). Just like Peter, Paul quotes directly from Hosea 1:10f to speak of his work in calling the Gentiles (Romans 9:24-26). For Paul, the conversion of the Gentiles was the fulfillment of Hosea.[31]

Finally, in regards to the wedding promised by Hosea, we go to the book of Revelation. In Revelation 18, we find the destruction of the city Babylon, the city, "where the Lord was slain." Then, at that destruction, it was announced, "Let us be glad and rejoice, and give Him glory, for the marriage of the Lamb has come, and His wife has made herself ready." What we have here is, *the scepter was now departed from Judah*, and the time of the wedding, promised in the Old Testament scriptures, had arrived. God was keeping His promises to Israel.[32]

The point is that John saw the wedding taking place when the unfaithful city was stoned and burned (the punishment for adultery), and he saw it happening very soon, "The Spirit and the Bride say, 'Come!'" (Revelation 22:17). Now, if John, anticipating the Wedding promised by Hosea for the last days of Israel, said it was time for the Wedding, then assuredly, the last days of Israel were present. Further, if John saw the Wedding taking place at the time of the destruction of the city, "where the Lord was slain," then this also demands that the last days are associated with Israel, and not the church.

So, the promise of Hosea is a powerful aid in identifying the last days. The prophecy concerns Israel and her last days. We have the testimony of Jesus, Paul, Peter and John, that the prophecy of Hosea was being fulfilled in their lifetime, well after the last days of Israel were supposedly postponed. Their use of Hosea *proves* however, that they were indeed living in Israel's last days, and therefore the idea that Israel's last days are now present, or will be shortly, is wrong.

JOEL 2:28-32

Another of the most important of all the Old Testament prophecies of the last days is Joel 2:28-32:

"And it shall come to pass afterward, that I will pour out my spirit upon all flesh; and your sons and your daughters shall prophesy, your old men shall dream dreams, your young men shall see visions: And also upon the servants and upon the handmaids in those days will I pour out my spirit. And I will shew wonders in the heavens and in the earth, blood, and fire, and pillars of smoke. The sun shall be turned into darkness, and the moon into blood, before the great and terrible day of the LORD come. And it shall come to pass, that whosoever shall call on the name of the LORD shall be delivered: for in mount Zion and in Jerusalem shall be deliverance, as the LORD hath said, and in the remnant whom the LORD shall call." (KJV)

This is an important prophecy, not only for what it says, but for what the New Testament says about it.

At this juncture you need to be aware, if you aren't already, that the modern prophecy pundits like LaHaye, Jeffrey, Jack Van Impe, and others, do not believe that Joel's prophecy has been fulfilled. Ice says that Joel:28f will be fulfilled during the Tribulation period leading directly to the Second Coming and of course, he believes this is still future. (*Prophecy*, 137) The reason the millennial camp does not believe this prophecy has been fulfilled is multi-faceted. They do not believe the kingdom was established in the first century, and since the outpouring of the Spirit was to result in the kingdom, then Joel could not have been fulfilled.

The trouble with saying that Joel 2 has never been fulfilled is that the inspired Biblical text says otherwise. Notice that in Acts 1:4f, Jesus told the disciples to go into Jerusalem and not leave, "but to wait for the Promise of the Father." The promise they were to wait for was the Holy Spirit that had been promised by John the Immerser (v. 5). And this is what is so important about this. The promise made by John, of the outpouring of the Spirit, was the promise of Joel 2.

So, Jesus, in Acts 1, promised the disciples that Joel was about to be fulfilled. This is confirmed by the fact that as soon as Jesus told them they were about to receive the Spirit, they immediately asked: "Will you at this time restore the kingdom to Israel?" (Acts 1:6f). The promise of the Spirit prompted the question about the kingdom. The reason is simple, the outpouring of the Spirit would result in the establishment of the kingdom. That is why, when Jesus said they were about to receive the Spirit, that they asked, "Will you at this time restore the kingdom to Israel."

The flow of the text, and the statements made in Acts 1 are a powerful refutation of the idea that the kingdom offer had been withdrawn from Israel. If the kingdom had been postponed, the disciples certainly did not think so. They understood Jesus' promise of the Spirit was the promise of the kingdom. Notice again what happened. Jesus said, "Go into Jerusalem and wait until you receive the promise of the Spirit foretold by John" (and Joel, the source of the promise). The disciples, upon hearing that the reception of the Spirit was this imminent, asked if Jesus was now restoring the kingdom. The relationship between the promise of the Spirit and establishment of the kingdom is undeniable and inextricable. If the kingdom offer had been withdrawn, why was Jesus saying that the Spirit was about to be poured out in fulfillment of the kingdom prophecies?

It is popular among non-millennial writers to say the disciples were still confused about the nature of the kingdom, and still had an earthly kingdom in mind, but that Jesus corrected their confusion. This simply is not true. Jesus had *opened the minds of the disciples* to understand the scriptures (Luke 24:25f, 44f). Furthermore, he spent 40 days with them, "speaking of the things pertaining to the kingdom of God" (Acts 1:4). Are we to suppose that even though the Master opened their eyes to understand the scriptures, and then instructed them for 40 days, *that they still didn't get it?*[33] Was Jesus that bad of an instructor that he could not get his point across, or were the disciples so hard headed that even after *being enlightened and instructed* by Jesus that they did not understand?

In Acts 1:6, the question is about the *time of the kingdom*, not the *nature* of the kingdom. Not only this, but Jesus' answer was about *time*, "It is not for you to know the *times*," not about the *nature* of the kingdom. If the disciples did not yet understand the nature of the kingdom, why didn't Jesus correct them? Why did he not express disappointment or discouragement as he did in his ministry on the occasions when the disciples clearly did not understand what he said? (Cf. John 6; 14, etc.).

Acts 1 sets the stage for understanding the events of Acts 2. Jesus' instruction of the disciples in regard to the kingdom and the Spirit were couched in unmistakable terms of imminence. He instructed them not to leave Jerusalem, but to, "wait for the Promise of the Father." The promise was the promise of the Spirit found in Joel 2. In other words, Jesus was telling the disciples not to leave Jerusalem because the promise of Joel 2 was about to be fulfilled!

With these thoughts in mind, we turn now to the day of Pentecost, 50 days after Jesus' passion, and after the enlightenment of the apostles, and the 40 days of instruction concerning the kingdom. The apostles and disciples were gathered together as instructed by Jesus, awaiting the outpouring of the Holy Spirit in fulfillment of Joel 2. Acts 2:1-4 records the awesome events of that day:

"When the day of Pentecost was fully come, they were all with one accord in one place. And suddenly there came a sound from heaven as of a rushing mighty wind, and it filled all the house where they were sitting. And there appeared unto them cloven tongues like as of fire, and it sat upon each of them. And they were all filled with the Holy Ghost, and began to speak with other tongues, as the Spirit gave them utterance." (KJV)

The response of the audience that day was mixed, to say the least. Some accused the apostles of being drunk. However, Peter stood up, and gave one of the most famous speeches in history:

"But Peter, standing up with the eleven, lifted up his voice, and said unto them, 'Ye men of Judea, and all ye that dwell at Jerusalem, be this known unto you, and hearken to my words: For these are not drunken, as ye suppose, seeing it is but the third hour of the day. But this is that which was spoken by the prophet Joel; 'And it shall come to pass in the last days, saith God, I will pour out of my Spirit upon all flesh: and your sons and your daughters shall prophesy, and your young men shall see visions, and your old men shall dream dreams.'"

Please take special note of Peter's emphatic words, "This is that which was spoken by the prophet Joel." Remember that we pointed out above that the millennialists do not believe that Joel 2 has been fulfilled. Jerry Falwell, evangelist and founder of Liberty University, wrote a column on World Net Daily, saying, "God has promised a greater outpouring of His Spirit in these last days before Jesus returns." He then cites Joel 2:28f. Falwell clearly does not believe that the events of Acts 2 were the fulfillment of Joel's promise. Arnold Fruchtenbaum goes so far as to say that, "Virtually nothing that happened in Acts 2 is predicted in Joel 2."[34] This is strange.

Joel said certain events would transpire *in the last days*. Jesus and the New Testament writers said they were living *in the last days* (Hebrews 1:1; 1 Peter 1:20, 1 John 2:18). Joel said the Holy Spirit would be poured out, and the Spirit was poured out on Pentecost. Joel said when the Spirit was poured out, miraculous manifestations would follow. In Acts 2 the Spirit was poured out and the apostles miraculously spoke in languages they had never spoken. Joel said that the Spirit would be poured out on all flesh, and Peter said the Spirit could be received not only by the Jews but on the Gentiles, i.e. "those afar off" (Acts 2:39). Joel said when the Spirit was poured out, it would be a sign of the Day of the Lord, and Peter warned his audience to, "Save yourselves from this untoward generation." Joel said that when the Spirit was poured out, anyone could call on the name of the Lord for salvation. On the day of Pentecost, the Spirit was poured out, and the gospel began to be preached for the salvation of all men. Joel said "in the last days" the Spirit would be poured out, and Peter said "This is that which was spoken by the prophet Joel!"

> You cannot make Peter's, "This is that" mean, "This is _not_ that!"

Don't you find it disturbing that some Bible students are willing to say that Peter was wrong, or that he was mistaken? Peter did not say, "This is _like_ what will eventually happen." He did not say, "This is a type, or foretaste of what will happen in the future." He _did not say_, "The events of this day prove that the Spirit can be, and will be, eventually, poured out when the last days finally arrive in the distant future." And, Peter _did not say_, "Virtually nothing that is happening here today was foretold by Joel 2." Peter _did say_, "This is that which was spoken by the prophet Joel."

Ask yourself, if Peter _wanted_ to say that Joel's prophecy was being fulfilled that day, would his words, "This is that which was spoken by the prophet Joel," convey that message? If not, what is there in, "This is that," that says it was _not_ the fulfillment of Joel? It is a perversion of scripture to turn Peter's, "This is that" into, "This is _not_ that!"

So what does this mean? It means that the last days foretold by Joel were present on Pentecost. And if the last days foretold by Joel were present on Pentecost, then plainly, the countdown of Israel's last days had not been suspended a year earlier, or even two months earlier. This is tremendously important, for remember that the millennialists insist that Israel's last days ended in Matthew 12, or, at the latest, with Jesus' triumphant entry into Jerusalem in Matthew 21. The one and the only reason why millennialists are willing to blatantly deny that Joel was being fulfilled on Pentecost is because if Joel's last days were present, then the house of cards called millennialism crumbles to the ground!

Joel said that in the last days, Israel's last days, the Spirit would be poured out. The Spirit was poured out on Pentecost 2000 years ago, and Peter, the inspired apostle said, "This is that which was spoken by the prophet Joel." This means that the last days are not in the future, and it means we are not living in the last days today. Peter confined his last days discussion to his generation, "Save yourselves from this untoward generation" (Acts 2:40). In spite of the fact that men such as Lindsay, LaHaye, Ice and others confidently affirm that Joel will one day be fulfilled, the Bible unequivocally affirms that the last days were present in the first century, and consummated in that generation. We are not in the last days, and that is good news!

SUMMARY TO THIS POINT

What have we seen to this point? We have seen that the key Old Testament prophecies of the last days have to do with Israel's last days, and not the last days of time, and not to the entirety of the Christian Age. The importance of this cannot be over-emphasized, for to mis-identify the last days is to mis-apply the Biblical doctrine of the last things. More about that in other works.[35]

We have seen that the doctrine of the last days is tied to the judgment of Israel for shedding the blood of God's righteous, and that both the Old and New Testaments place the time of this judgment at the fall of Jerusalem in A.D. 70.

THE END HAS COME!

Now that we have seen the framework for the last days, we can move on to the confirmation that the last days are in the past, not the present, and not the future. This should be of great comfort to anyone to know that the horrendous events of the last days are past. We can't develop this at length here, so see our other works, but the realization that the last days have come and gone, and that the future can be, (*and should be!*), bright, should be a great comfort to believers. Instead of the gloom and doom message that says the world has to get worse and worse, and that believers can't do anything about it–"You don't polish brass on a sinking ship!"-- believers need to realize it is past time to be the "salt and light," and get out and get involved! It is time for the church to stop retreating, and start going to war as it once did, when it was confident that it is the Word of God that changes lives, and the world. The world doesn't need to *end* to improve, it needs to improve by the power of the Word of God!

It is time for the church to stop retreating, and start engaging the enemy as it once did, confident that the Word of God changes lives, and the world. **Onward, Christian soldiers!**

With that said, we need to confirm the points above by taking note of the incredible sense of the nearness of the end in the first century, and see how that contrasts with the Old Testament.

The Old Testament never says that the prophets and their contemporaries were living in the last days. When the prophets spoke of the last days, they were always far off. In direct contrast, the New Testament writers always said that the last days *foretold by the Old Testament prophets* were present! And, this is important, the New Testament writers never anticipated any other "last days" than those foretold in the Old Covenant prophecies. Let's take a closer look at some of these passages.

Since we examined Joel and Acts immediately above, let's start there again. It will be noted in the book of Joel that there were events that were near when Joel wrote (Joel 2:1, 10), but that the last days were still far off (Joel 2:28). In other words, Joel did not, in spite of what many say, believe the end was coming soon. Some events were near, but the last days were not. However, when we come to Acts 2, as we have seen, Peter affirmed, "This is that which was spoken by the prophet Joel." This contrast between what Joel believed about the presence of the last days, and what the New Testament writers said has to be honored.

At this point it will be good to re-introduce what Peter had to say about the last days. In 1 Peter 1, the apostle was speaking about the last days, and the salvation promised by the Old Testament prophets who foretold the last days. He said:

"Of this salvation the prophets have inquired and searched carefully, who prophesied of the grace that would come to you, searching what, or what manner of time, the Spirit of Christ who was in them was indicating when He testified beforehand of the glories that would follow. To them it was revealed that, not to themselves, but to us they were ministering the things which now have been reported to you by the Holy Spirit sent from heaven–things angels desire to look into." (1 Peter 1:10-12)

First, Peter was speaking of the salvation that the Old Testament prophets said would come in the last times (1 Peter 1:5, 10).

Second, Peter said the Old Testament prophets were told that the prophecies were not for their day. This means that the prophets did not think they were living in the last days. This is very important. Notice the contrast. The Old Testament prophets wrote over 500 years before Peter, and were informed that the fulfillment of their prophecies, *in the last days,* were not for their day.

We are told by our dispensational friends that those Old Testament prophets actually spoke of *our* generation. However, if the Old Testament prophets knew that their prophecies were not for their day, and if the fulfillment was not for Peter's day either, then why did Peter say those Old Testament prophets ministered to his generation? Why did Peter not say that the former prophets knew their prophecies were not for them, and, "we realize they are not for our day either"? Why didn't Peter say the prophets spoke of things that were still not for his day, but for a far distant future generation? The Old Testament prophets said the last days were far off, why couldn't Peter say the same? Instead, he said he was living in the last days foretold by those Old Covenant prophets.

It has been 4 times longer from Peter to the present than it was from the last of the Old Covenant prophets to Peter. Peter said the Old Covenant prophets knew their predictions were far off, but were for his day "unto us they did minister." But, Peter could not truthfully say that unless the last days foretold by the prophets, the last days of Israel, were truly present in his generation.

Third, Peter emphatically says that while the Old Prophets were informed that they were not living in the days of fulfillment, that the salvation they foretold for the last days was, *when Peter wrote*, "ready to be revealed in the last times" (v. 5). The word translated "ready" means that it was about to be revealed.

Fourth, Peter states in the clearest way, that he was living in the last days, and that the end was near. In verse 20 he said Christ was manifested "in these last days." That meant Peter's generation, because that is when Jesus was manifested. In 1 Peter 4:5, 7, and 17, the apostle states in some of the clearest language in the Bible that the time of the end was very near when he wrote.

Fifth, all of this means that we must honor Peter's statements that the last days foretold by the prophets were present. This is important because if the last days foretold by the Old Testament prophets were present when Peter wrote, it was the last days of *Israel*. As we have seen, the Old Testament prophets do not predict the end of time, or the end of the Christian Age. But, if the last days of Israel were present when Peter wrote, circa 63-65 A.D., the premillennial doctrine is false.

We cannot fail to note, again, that the millennialists deny that the Old Testament had anything at all to say about the Church Age. Spargimino says, "The Hebrew prophets knew nothing of this phase," of God's plan. (*Anti-Prophets*, 195). Well, if the Old Testament prophets knew nothing about the Church Age, and wrote only of Israel and her promises, then when Peter says that his generation was experiencing what the prophets foretold, this means, unequivocally, that what was happening in Peter's generation was the events of *Israel's last days*.

The millennialist cannot respond by saying that Peter was writing about the *spiritual blessings* of the Abrahamic Covenant, and not the promises to national Israel. This does not solve the problem. If the Old Testament prophets foretold the spiritual blessings of the Abrahamic Covenant, then since the spiritual blessings of the Abrahamic Covenant are in Christ and the church (Galatians 3:26-29), it is patently obvious that the Old Testament prophets did in fact predict the Church Age.

It is wrong to apply Peter's statements to events and times 2000 years removed from him. The last days were Peter's contemporary generation. They were the last days foretold by the Old Testament prophets. They were the last days of Israel, not the last days of the Christian Age.

Not only did Peter believe that he was living in the critical last days period, the other apostles and inspired writers taught the same thing. Notice just a few of the many passages, inspired by the Holy Spirit, that state the last days were present in the first century.

1.) We call attention again to Acts 2:15f. Peter quotes Joel 2:28f. Joel said in the last days the Spirit would be poured out. Peter said, "This is that which was spoken by the prophet Joel." There could not be a clearer affirmation that the anticipated last days had arrived.

2.) Acts 3:19-24. Peter is again the speaker, and he says that the Old Testament prophets "spoke of these days." Peter said the Old Testament prophets foretold the days in which he was living. He did not say that they spoke of the days 2000 years in the future from Peter. He said, "All the prophets, from Samuel and those who follow, as many as have spoken, foretold these days" (v. 24). Now, since the Old Testament prophets spoke of the last days, and since Peter said they foretold the time in which he was living, then this means that the time in which Peter was living was the last days foretold by the Old Testament prophets.

3.) 1 Corinthians 10:11–This is a critical passage for understanding the framework of the last days. We will spend a bit of time here.

> "Now all these things happened to them as examples, and they were written for our admonition, upon whom the ends of the ages have arrived." (1 Corinthians 10:11)

This passage is significant since Paul says the end of the age had arrived. He clearly was not saying that the end of the Christian Age had arrived. He was not saying that *the end of time* had arrived, or else he was patently wrong. The question that needs to be asked is, the end of what age had arrived?

The Jews believed in only two ages, and the New Testament writers concurred in that belief. See the special study, *The Age To Come*, at the end of this book. It is a response to Ice's contention that the Church Age has displaced the age of Israel as "this age."

The Jews believed in "this age" and the "age to come." Their "this age" was the age of Moses and the Law, and the "age to come" was the age of Messiah and the New Covenant. The age of Moses and the Law was to end (Hebrews 8:13), while the age of Messiah and the New Covenant was to be eternal (Matthew 24:35). Given this view of the ages, it is patently false to interpret such passages as Matthew 24:2-3 as predictions or inquiries about the end of the Christian Age.

Two Greek words help us appreciate the Corinthian passage. The first word is translated as *ends*, and is the word *tele*, from *telos*. This word often means termination, or end as we often think of it, e. g. "the end of all things has drawn near" (1 Peter 4:7). However, this is not the whole story. Even when the idea of termination is dominant, there is often another idea present, and that is that the *goal* of that which was being terminated has been reached. (See the Lexicons for all the derivatives of *teleios*).

Thus, to say that something was coming to an end indicated that it had reached its prophetic goal. Paul said that Christ was, "the end of the law for righteousness, to all those who believe" (John 1:17f; Romans 10:4). Not only was Jesus the end of the Law objectively, since he brought that Old Covenant Age to its end, but he was the *goal* of that Old World. As Galatians 3:23f says, the Law was a guardian of those under that System to bring them to Christ, and "the faith." When that system was fully set in place, the Law was supposed to end. Thus, the end (*tele*) of the Law was not only the *termination* of the Law, but the *goal* of the Law.

For Paul to say that the end of the ages had arrived was an incredible statement! But, he did not stop with the word *tele*, he spoke of his contemporary brethren as those, "upon whom the ends of the ages has come." When he said that the end of the ages had come, he used another distinctive word. He uses the perfect tense of *katantao*. This word is used some twelve times in the New Testament, and it means, "to arrive at something, to arrive at a destination"[36] This word is used, normally, to speak of arriving at a destination of travel.[37]

Katantao is used four times in a theological sense.

First, Paul says the twelve tribes were serving God night and day, hoping to "come" (*katantao*) unto the resurrection (Acts 26:7).

Second, Paul chided the Corinthians for being puffed up with pride. They thought of themselves as the "all in all" of Christianity and maturity. However, Paul asks the rhetorical question, "Did the gospel come unto you only?" (1 Corinthians 14:36). This was Paul's way of saying that they were not the goal of the preaching of the gospel. The gospel had other "destinations" beyond Corinth.

Third, *katantao* is used by the same apostle when he says that the charismata were given to equip the church to do the work of the ministry, "until we all come (*katantao*) to the unity of the faith, to the measure of the stature of the fullness of Christ" (Ephesians 4:13). The unity of the faith was the goal anticipated by the praxis of the charismata. And, it was the arrival of that unity of the faith that would not only be the goal, but the termination of the charismata (1 Corinthians 13:8f). Termination and goal go hand in hand here.

Fourth, in Philippians 3:11 Paul said that it was his fervent desire to "attain" (*katantao*) to the resurrection from the dead. Just like resurrection was the goal of Israel's eschatological and Messianic aspirations, Paul, who preached nothing but the hope of Israel (Acts 24; 25; 26; 28), said the resurrection was his desired destination.

With the use of *telos* and *katantao*, Paul was undeniably saying that not only was the termination of the previous ages at hand, but *the goal of all previous ages was being achieved!* This has powerful implications.

WHAT WAS THE GOAL OF THE AGES?

To see the implications of Paul's statement, we need to remind ourselves of *the goal of the ages.* What was it that all previous ages anticipated, predicted, and pointed toward? The answer can be couched in different terms.

The goal of the previous ages was the *New Creation* (Isaiah 65-66), and repeatedly, Paul taught that the New Creation was a reality in Christ: "If any man be in Christ, he is a New Creation, old things are passed away, behold, all things are become new!" (2 Corinthians 5:17, see Ephesians 4; Colossians 3, etc.)

The goal of the ages was *the Age to come* (Luke 20:33f), when "this age" would come to an end (Matthew 13:39-40).

The goal of the previous ages was *the New Covenant World of the Messiah* (Galatians 3:23f). The Law, as we have seen briefly above, was only a tutor, a guardian, of those under it, "until the Seed should come to whom the promises were made." It cannot be argued that the Law ended with the mere appearance of Jesus, for this would indicate that the Law passed when He was born. The coming under consideration has to be His coming to fully establish the New Covenant and remove the Old.

The goal of all the previous ages, and *God's eternal purpose,* was the arrival of the Age in which, "He might gather together in one all things in

Christ, both which are in heaven and which are on earth–in Him" (Ephesians 1:10). This was to be accomplished in the "fulness of times" and, as we know from Ephesians 2:11f, was being accomplished, not in a restoration of national Israel, but in the body of Christ, the church. We also know that Jesus appeared in the fulness of time (Galatians 4:4), and therefore, the time for the goal of the ages to be realized had come.

The destination anticipated by the previous ages was, in a word, *the kingdom*, and this is why 1 Corinthians 10:11 is so important. It must be remembered that the millennialist does not believe that the Church Age was anticipated by the previous ages. In fact, according to leading millennialists, the Church Age, established by Jesus through his blood, *was a total mystery to the previous Ages!* Pentecost says, "The existence of this present age which was to interrupt God's established program with Israel, was a mystery (Matthew 13:11)."[38] He also adds,

> "The existence of an entirely new age which only interrupts temporarily God's program for Israel, is one of the strongest arguments for the premillennial position. It is necessary for one who rejects that interpretation to prove that the church itself is the consummation of God's program."(136)

Finally, on page 137, Pentecost says, "The concept must stand that this whole age with its program was not revealed in the Old Testament, but constitutes a new program and a new line of revelation in this present age...It has been illustrated how this whole age existed in the mind of God without having been revealed in the Old Testament."

So, here is what we have: Paul said *the goal of the previous ages* had arrived. However, what was occurring when Paul wrote, the age that was breaking in, *was the Church Age.* According to the millennialists the Kingdom Age, *which is not the Church Age*, is the goal of all the previous ages. However, since Paul said that what was happening when he wrote was the goal of the previous ages, then it cannot be true that the restoration of national Israel is in fact, the goal of all previous ages. And of course, this means that the millennial view is fundamentally flawed.

If it is true that the Church Age was the goal of the previous ages, then the church is not a "temporary interruption" of God's kingdom plans. It is undeniably true that Paul says that what was happening in his day, through his ministry–and don't forget that he proclaimed the "hope of Israel"–was in fact that goal, the destiny of all previous ages. Therefore, it must be true that the Church Age was the fulfillment of the "hope of Israel," and was the goal of all previous ages. In a word, if the Church was the goal of the previous ages, the millennial doctrine is false.

When Paul says that the goal of the previous ages had arrived, this has incredible application for the term "last days." It must be remembered that the kingdom, God's promise to Israel, was to be established in the last days (Isaiah 2:2). Paul of course, affirmed that the time of the end was near (1 Corinthians 7:26f; Philippians 4:5, etc.). Now, if Paul affirmed that the time of the end was near, and that the goal of the previous ages had arrived, then this can only mean that the last days foretold by the Old Testament prophets were present. Of course, the implications for the millennial view, given this reality, are staggering since they deny that Israel's last days were in existence after Matthew 12. However, the fact that Paul says the end was near, and that the goal of the previous ages had arrived, means that the last days of Israel were in fact present when he wrote, and essentially, this destroys the entire millennial house of cards!

Paul's statement in 1 Corinthians 10:11 also has implications for the amillennial and postmillennial views. Both of these paradigms insist that the Christian Age will one day end, giving way to the eternal Age to come. This view is flawed in its posit of a different Age to come than that anticipated by the prophets and Jesus.

However, these futurist views violate the fact that as the goal of all previous ages, the Christian Age has *no end!* Daniel was told that when the kingdom that was to be established in the days of Rome was established, that it would *never pass away*; or be destroyed (Daniel 2:44; 7:13-14). However, both the amillennial and postmillennial schools insist that one day the Church Age will end, giving way to the Age to come.

The fact that Paul uses two distinctive words (*telos* and *katantao*), to speak of what was happening in his day is a powerful testimony to the place of the church in God's Scheme of Redemption. The blood bought Church of Jesus is and was the goal of the previous ages!

Unless one can demonstrate that Paul had something other than the Church, the body of Christ in mind when he spoke of the goal of the ages, then *the Church was the anticipated destiny of the previous ages*. This destroys the millennial doctrine that the church is a "temporary interruption" of God's kingdom plan.

Look again at Pentecost's comments. He says the strongest argument for the premillennial view is the idea that the church was not, "the consummation of God's program." He is saying that *the Church Age is not the goal of the previous ages*. Well, unless Paul had something other than the church in mind when he said that the goal of the ages *had arrived*, then 1 Corinthians 10:11 proves beyond doubt that the church really is, "the consummation of God's program." This means that the last days foretold by the prophets were present when Paul wrote.

4.) Hebrews 1:1–The inspired writer tells us that Jesus appeared "in these last days." The author was speaking here of the personal ministry of Jesus. However, he also knew that, although it was, "nigh unto passing away" (Hebrews 8:13), the Old Covenant World of Israel had not yet passed. He was still in those last days.

5.) Hebrews 9:26– The writer says that Jesus appeared in the end of the ages. He uses the identical term used by the disciples when they asked about the "end of the age" in Matthew 24:3. More about this later. It is clear that Jesus did not appear at the end of the Christian Age, isn't it? It is also obvious that he did not appear *at the end of time*. However, he did appear in the last days, the last generation, of the Old Covenant World of Israel (Galatians 4:4).

6.) 1 Peter 1:10-12; 20; 4:7– Peter is an incredibly significant epistle in regard to the last days. A great deal could be said, but we will keep our comments brief. Please take note of several facts.

First, Peter said that the salvation he was writing about was, "ready to be revealed" (1 Peter 1:5). The Greek word that he uses for "ready" means just that. It has the idea of preparedness and nearness. It is like a bride all dressed up and "prepared" for the wedding. When that bride is all dressed up, that wedding is near!

Second, Peter said that the salvation was ready to be revealed "in the last time," and then states clearly that he was living in "these last times" (v. 20). These are not two different last times periods.

Third, Peter said that the salvation he was writing about was foretold by the Old Testament prophets. Thus, the last days that Peter was writing about, the days in which he was living, were the last times foretold by the Old Testament prophets. This is significant because, if you will remember, the millennialists insist that the Old Testament foretold the last days of Israel *exclusively*. So, if Peter was saying that the time in which he was living was the time foretold by the Old Testament prophets, and the Old Testament prophets spoke only of the last days of Israel, then Peter was affirming that he was living in the last days of Israel.

Of course, as we have shown, this is devastating to the millennial view because they deny that Israel's last days were in existence when Peter wrote. They insist that Israel's last days countdown was suspended in Matthew 12, when Jesus perceived the hardheartedness of the Jews.

Fourth, Peter clearly affirms that the Old Testament prophets were told that the things they were predicting were not for their days (v. 11-12). This means that the prophets knew they were not living in the last days.

Fifth, while Peter says that the Old Testament prophets knew that their predictions were not for their day, he affirms that what they foretold was for his generation (v. 12. cf. Matthew 13:17). This can hardly be overemphasized. Peter's contrast between the Old Testament prophets and his generation must be honored. This means that when God told the Old Testament prophets that what they were foreseeing was not for their day, but was far off (Daniel 10; 12), that the language of time was to be taken at face value. A long time meant *a long time*. In contrast, Peter says that what was once far off to the prophets was "now," and that is *Peter's* "now," not *ours*, "ready to be revealed." Shouldn't we honor Peter's statements?

Peter tells us Jesus was manifested "in these last times" and, "The end of all things has drawn near" (Literal translation). So, Peter, like Jesus and Paul, believed that the last days were in existence when he wrote. He believed he was living in the critical time of the end. Was he wrong? Or are those who say we are in the last times today the ones that are wrong?

7.) 1 John 2:18– We have here one of the most emphatic, the clearest expressions that the last days were present in the first century that we could find. John, the inspired apostle said, "Little children, it is the last hour. As you have heard that anti-Christ should come, even now there are many anti-Christs. Thereby you know it is the last hour."

This verse is critical, not only because of what it does say, but because of what it does not say. John does not say, "You know that you are living in the Christian Age because anti-Christs have come." Yet, that is the way many read it. However, is *a denial of Jesus as Messiah the identifying characteristic of the Christian Age?*

John did not say, "It is the last age." Yet, some would have us believe this is what he meant. Are we to believe that the word "hour" is being used in such an unusual way? When we examine John's gospel, we discover that he uses the word "hour" in a critical, imminent sense. He records several instances in which Jesus said, "My hour has not yet come," or, "For this hour I came into the world" etc. Not only that, he uses the term *last hour*, or "the hour is coming," to refer to the climax of the last days (John 5:28-29; John 12:48f). In other words, "the last hour" in John did not designate a long period of time. It meant the climax of the last days. Thus, when John said, "It is the last hour!," this is a powerful declaration that the last days were not only present when he wrote, they were rapidly coming to a close.

We must take note here that some try to delineate between *the last days* and *the last day*. This is done to hold onto some traditional views. However, this view is untenable. Would not the last days have a "last day?" If not, why not? To suggest that the *last days* is a referent to the last days of Israel, but then to insist that the term last *day*, must refer to the end of the Christian Age, is to create a dichotomy not found in the Bible. This is proven in many scriptures.

First, in Matthew 24, Jesus spoke of "those days" (v. 19, 22), that would lead up to the final day of the end of the age (v. 29f).

Second, the same "days" leading up to "the day" is presented in Luke 17:26-30. Yet it is plain from the text that the passage has nothing to do with any supposed end of time scenario, because in the text, Jesus told them that if they were on their rooftops in the end times, they were to flee! Now, if the last days are a time as described by most futurists, there would be no chance to flee. Clearly though, Jesus did not agree with these traditional views of the end times, for he said it would be possible to flee.

Third, as we have seen, the time of the vindication of the martyrs was to be at the end of the last days. This is admitted by all. Yet, the attempt is made to delineate between the last day versus the last days. Well, if the vindication of the martyrs was to occur at the end of Jesus' generation, at the climax of the last days in the judgment of Israel, and if the vindication of the martyrs is inextricably linked with the last day, then there is no way, scripturally, to divorce the last *day* from the last *days*.

Fourth, the term *last hour* would be linked with *the last day*, would it not? How could a person claim that the last day, would not be associated with the last hour? In John's gospel and in his epistle they certainly are linked. In John's gospel the climax of the last days is the *last hour*, when the martyrs are rewarded (John 5:28-29). Then, in 1 John 2:18, that same author said, "Little children it is the last hour, and as you have heard that anti-christ should come, even now there are many anti-christs, thereby you know it is the last hour."

So, John, who wrote of the last day and the last hour, emphatically said that the last hour was so near, so pressing, that he could say it had arrived. Thus, it is simply not valid to argue that the *last days* refer to the last days of Israel, but that the *last day* must be future. The attempt to divorce the last hour and the last days from the last day is an exercise in theological futility. For John the inspired apostle, the end was present.

Many other New Testament passages say, in plain language, that the end of the age, or the time of the end, was to occur in that generation. Jesus said the end was to come in the lifetime of his disciples (Matthew 10:22-23; Matthew 16:27-28), and the authors of the epistles likewise echoed this fact (1 Corinthians 15:50-51; 1 Thessalonians 4:15, 17, etc.).

The challenge for the modern day Bible reader is to cut through all the hype, the sensationalism, and the rhetoric of men like Hagee,[39] LaHaye, Jeffrey, Van Impe, and the like, and listen to the inspired writers for a change. Listen to what *Jesus* had to say about when the end was coming.

Listen to what *Peter* said about how near the end was. Listen to *Paul* as he affirmed that his first century audience would live to see the end. Listen to the inspired, authoritative *Word of God*, that says the last days were in the first century, and that the time of the end was not supposed to be the end of time, or the destruction of earth, but the end of the Old Covenant World of Israel. When we listen to the inspired Word of God, we will not be disappointed. When we listen to the television prophecy "experts" we are doomed to disappointment and disillusionment.

THE PROPHECIES OF DANIEL AND THE LAST DAYS: DANIEL 2:28F

As promised, we now turn to the book of Daniel to examine its prophecies to help us identify the last days. The information in Daniel is extremely helpful and will confirm our contention that the last days were related to the last days of Israel.

The king of Babylon, Nebuchadnezzar, had a dream. He called his soothsayers and psychics in and told them they had to tell *him the content of his dream*, and then the interpretation. You can imagine the consternation among those would be prophets. They knew they could not tell him the content of his dream. But if they didn't, they were about to die! Finally, God's prophet, Daniel, was called in, and he not only told Nebuchadnezzar his dream, he gave him the interpretation! The year was circa B. C. 603 (Daniel 2:1).

The prophecy of Daniel 2, the vision of the great image made of gold, silver, brass, and iron, is one of the great prophecies of the Old Testament. Daniel told Nebuchadnezzar: "There is a God in heaven who reveals secrets, and He has made known to King Nebuchadnezzar what will be in the latter days."

The king's vision was about a great image of a man: "The head was gold, the chest and arms of silver, its belly and thighs of bronze, and its legs of iron and partly of clay" (Daniel 2:32f). What is important about this prophecy is that we know the beginning point, and the ending point. The beginning point is the kingdom of Babylon, Daniel said to Nebuchadnezzar:

"You, O, king, are a king of kings. For the God of heaven has given you a kingdom, power, strength and glory...but after you shall arise another king, inferior to yours, then another, a third kingdom of bronze, which shall rule over all the earth, and the fourth kingdom shall be as strong as iron, inasmuch as iron breaks in pieces and shatters everything, and like iron that crushes, that kingdom will break in pieces and crush all the others."

Among conservative Bible students, the countdown of the four kingdoms is almost universally agreed to be, Babylon, Medo-Persian, Greece, and Rome.[40] It was to be in the days of the last kingdom, *Rome*, that, "the God of heaven shall set up a kingdom which shall never be destroyed" (Daniel 2:44). This was not to be a man-made, earthly kingdom, but a kingdom, "not made with hands" (v. 34). So, Daniel tells us that in the days of the Roman empire, *in the last days*, God would establish the kingdom. *This means that the last days cannot extend beyond the days of the Roman Empire.* Let's notice several facts.

First, the prophecy relates to *the promises of Israel*. The promise of the kingdom was a promise made to Israel (Isaiah 2-4), as we have seen. Daniel 2 is not a promise made to the church, about the end of time. It is a promise made to Israel, even though the vision was given to Nebuchadnezzar.

Second, take note that just like Isaiah said, the kingdom would be established *in the last days*. *It does not say* that the last days would begin with the establishment of the kingdom. It says the kingdom would be established *in the last days*.

Third, here is what we know for sure about Daniel's prediction, and what the New Testament has to say about it.

A.) Jesus appeared in the days of the Roman Empire (Luke 2:1),

B.) He appeared *in the last days* (Hebrews 1:1-2),

C.) He proclaimed: "The time is fulfilled, the kingdom of heaven is at hand!"

What did Jesus mean when he said, "The time is fulfilled?" What *time* was he referring to? The book of Daniel is the *only* prophetic book that purports to give a time for when the kingdom of God was to be established, and, according to widespread general belief, the time foretold by Daniel was present in the first century. One thing is for certain, *Jesus thought the time was right*, and the only way he could have thought that was if it agreed with prophecy.

This raises some serious issues. Jesus knew Daniel's prophecy better than anyone. If the time for establishing the kingdom, in fulfillment of Daniel 2 was not truly near, then why did Jesus say, "The time is fulfilled, the kingdom of heaven is at hand"? If there was to be a 2000 year gap between his day and a "Revived Roman Empire" when the kingdom would finally be established, why did Jesus offer the kingdom back then? If the kingdom cannot be established until Rome is restored, then Jesus was wrong to say the kingdom was near in the first century.

Fourth, note that in Daniel 2:44 (and chapter 7 see below), the kingdom of God is, in contrast to the other kingdoms, *eternal*. In chapter 2, the first four kingdoms pass away, they all had "last days." However, Daniel said the kingdom that Jehovah would establish would "never be destroyed." In other words, in contrast to the preceding four kingdoms that all had last days, *the kingdom of heaven would not have last days, because it will never pass away!* Likewise, in Daniel 7:13-14, Messiah would be given a kingdom that could *never pass away*, nor be destroyed, and again, this in contrast with the four kingdoms that would pass.

All futurists teach that the Christian Age will come to an end. Ice says, "The purpose for the Rapture is to end the Church Age."[41] It is evident however, based on the contrast between kingdoms that would and did have last days, that would and did *cease to exist*, that it is improper to speak of the last days of the Christian Age. How can you speak of the last days of the Christian Age, or the end of the Christian Age, when the Christian Age will never pass away?

It is worthwhile to take a brief trip to Daniel 7 since it confirms our comments above, and shows that the last days must be confined to the days of the Roman Empire. The prophecy of Daniel 7 was given later than that of chapter 2, and under Belshazzar, but still under the Babylonian Empire (Daniel 7:1). This was approximately B.C. 555-550. Daniel now sees a vision that spans the same historical vista, and predicted the same event, the establishment of the everlasting kingdom of the Messiah. He saw four beasts representative of four kingdoms, just like Nebuchadnezzar did.

In the days of the fourth empire, and remember that is *Rome*, another Little Horn arises who persecutes the saints (7:8, 25). However, the books are opened, the judgment is set, and the Little Horn is judged and destroyed (7:9-11). Here is the judgment of Revelation 20! However, there are a couple of things that are important to notice.

First, there is no way to get this prophecy beyond the days of the Roman Empire. The judgment of the Little Horn had to have occurred in the days of the Roman Empire!

Of course, we are told that the image of the beast actually included the *Revived Roman Empire,* because, after all, the man in the vision *had two legs.* Each of the legs represents one of the two stages of the Roman Empire. One leg represents first century Rome, the other represents the Revived Roman Empire of the (supposedly) present generation. Of course, this distorts the image. Shouldn't the image have had one leg longer than the other one. Weren't the legs of the same length in the vision? Weren't the legs side by side? What is there about a vision of a man that suggests that the legs represent two different things separated by two millennia?

The bottom line is, did Jesus know the prophecy of Daniel and the vision of the beast with the two legs? Did he know that the two legs supposedly represented a then present Roman Empire and a future Revived Roman Empire? And, did Jesus know of the vision of the Little Horn? Surely. Significantly, he came in the days of the fourth kingdom, as Daniel prophesied, and said the kingdom was near. Where, *anywhere* in the teaching of Jesus, did he ever indicate a future Revival of Rome? *Nowhere!* If Jesus knew that the Roman Empire was to pass away, in about 400 years, and 1600 years later be revived, before the kingdom could be established, why did he say, "The kingdom has drawn near"? Jesus' emphatic declaration that the kingdom was near in the first century is totally destructive to the idea of a Revived Roman Empire.

Furthermore, since the kingdom was to be given the Son of Man at the time of the judgment of the Little Horn (Daniel 7:15f), this means without a doubt that the judgment of the Little Horn was near in the first century, or else, Jesus was wrong when he said, "The time is fulfilled, the kingdom of heaven is at hand."

Jesus and the New Testament writers affirm, in the most unequivocal manner, that the persecutor of the saints was *Israel*, and that she was going to be judged when the books were opened (Matthew 23).

Second, since Daniel 7 and Daniel 2 are parallel, and since Daniel 2 says that these events belong to the "last days," then we must confine the last days to the Roman Empire.

Third, as we have just seen, Daniel 7 speaks of the *everlasting kingdom* of the Messiah, a kingdom that will never pass away, in contrast to the other, earthly kingdoms that would pass away. If Jesus came, and established the kingdom that would never be moved (, i.e. the *church* Hebrews 12:28), then it is improper to speak of the last days of the Church Age. How can you remove *the unshakeable kingdom of the church,* and establish another unshakeable kingdom?

Fourth, it is obvious, isn't it, that Daniel was telling Nebuchadnezzar that the events were far off? The rise and fall of four world kingdoms demands a lot of time, normally. The last days were hundreds of years away from Daniel and his contemporaries. They were not near. Thus, when Jesus and the New Testament writers said that the last days had arrived, we must take their word for it.

Fifth, there is not a hint, *not a word*, to suggest a *Revived Roman Empire*. If Daniel predicted a Revived Roman Empire, centuries removed from the days of Jesus, when the kingdom was actually supposed to be established, then Jesus did not know it, because he said, "The time is fulfilled, the kingdom of heaven is at hand!" If Daniel's prophecy contained a gap of two millennia, and Jesus did not know about it then he cannot be the Son of God.[42] If Daniel's prophecy contains a gap of two millennia, and Jesus knew of it, but proclaimed the nearness of the kingdom anyway, then he lied, for the kingdom was not near.

The doctrine of a Revived Roman Empire is a theological fabrication derived from the idea that the kingdom was not established when it was originally supposed to, the days of first century Rome. The idea that Jesus failed to do *what* he came to do, i.e. establish the kingdom, *when* he was supposed to, i.e. in the days of the fourth kingdom, is one of the most Christ dishonoring, scripture denying, skeptic encouraging doctrines ever created!

> **The teaching that Jesus failed to do *what* he came to do, i.e. establish the kingdom, *when* he was supposed to, i.e. in the days of Rome, is one of the most Christ dishonoring, scripture denying, skeptic encouraging doctrines ever created!**

Think about this. The Old Testament predicted *what* the Messiah would do, establish the kingdom. The millennial doctrine says he did not do it. The Old Testament predicted *when* the kingdom would be established, in the days of Rome, yet, per the millennial view *Jesus did not fulfill that prophecy either.* So, according to this doctrine, *Jesus failed on all accounts!* He did not fulfill any part of the Old Testament prophecies concerning the kingdom! Not the *what*, and not the *when*! *What kind of a Savior fails to keep his promises?*

Sixth, only by agreeing that *Jesus was right* when he said, "The time is fulfilled, the kingdom of heaven is at hand," and by then proclaiming that he kept his word, can we even begin to proclaim *the inspiration of Daniel.* If Daniel said the kingdom was to be established in the days of Rome, and it wasn't, then Daniel's prediction failed.

When we come to the New Testament times, we are dealing with the time of the Roman Empire (Luke 2:1), the last of the four empires foretold by Daniel. And in direct contrast to Daniel who said the last days were coming, Jesus said, "The time is fulfilled!" (Mark 1:15). The last days had arrived in the first century! What Daniel said was far off was now near.

DANIEL 9:24-27

Thomas Ice calls Daniel 9:24-27 "one of the most important prophecy passages in the whole Bible." (*End Times*, 307) There is no doubt that it is of critical importance. The context of the prophecy is this. Israel had been carried off into Babylonian Captivity almost 70 years before Daniel wrote. Daniel was familiar with the prophecy of Jeremiah 25:11-12, that said the captivity would last for 70 years. With that promise in mind, Daniel prayed to Jehovah to "remind" Him of the promise of deliverance. The Lord responded with a reminder of His faithfulness, and then gave the following prophecy:

> "Seventy weeks are determined upon thy people and upon thy holy city, to finish the transgression, and to make an end of sins, and to

make reconciliation for iniquity, and to bring in everlasting righteousness, and to seal up the vision and prophecy, and to anoint the most Holy. Know therefore and understand, that from the going forth of the commandment to restore and to build Jerusalem unto the Messiah the Prince shall be seven weeks, and threescore and two weeks: the street shall be built again, and the wall, even in troublous times. And after threescore and two weeks shall Messiah be cut off, but not for himself: and the people of the prince that shall come shall destroy the city and the sanctuary; and the end thereof shall be with a flood, and unto the end of the war desolations are determined." (KJV)

Several things are apparent about this prophecy.

First, it is about *Israel*. It is not about the end of the Christian Age. The prophecy is about Daniel's people and the holy city of Jerusalem.

Second, the prophecy is about the consummation of God's promises of salvation.

Third, the prophecy does not contain one word about the destruction of earth, the end of time, or the cessation of the present age. It is all about Israel.

Fourth, the prophecy terminates with the fate of Jerusalem climaxing in "the war" and in desolation. Remember the prophecy of Isaiah 3:25f, where Isaiah foretold the judgment of Israel in the last days in "the war." This would be when Israel would be judged for her blood guilt, and as we have seen, Jesus said Israel was to be judged for her blood guilt in his generation (Matthew 23:29f).

The normal interpretation of Daniel 9 is that the 70 Weeks are 490 years. Based on the idea that seventy sevens equals 490, we are to see each day as a year. Thus, 70 times seven equals 490 years. It is possible however, that this is not a referent to a mathematical calculation at all, but a symbolic referent to the grand Jubilee. The important thing to know is that the prophecy gives us the starting point, "from the command to restore and rebuild Jerusalem," and the ending point, "until the end, desolations are determined" (v. 27).

The end of the vision is the fall of Jerusalem in A.D. 70, "Seventy weeks are determined on your... *city*." Does it not make sense that when Daniel was told, "until the *end* desolations are determined," that the end in view is the end of the 70th Week? What other *end* is in view? There has been absolutely no mention of any so-called end of time. There has been no mention of the end of the church for sure. The only "end" in the text is the end of the 70ᵗʰ Week, and the only end in view is that concerning "the people and the city."

It would also be at the end of the 70 Weeks that Everlasting Righteousness would become a reality. Vision and Prophecy would be sealed up, consummated via fulfillment.[43] By that time, "the most holy" would be anointed, and atonement for sin would be made (cf. v. 24). In other words, the kingdom of heaven would be established at the end of the 70 Weeks.

The problem is that in the mind of the millennialists like LaHaye, Ice, Van Impe and others, the kingdom was not established at the end of the 490 years, in the way that they insist it should. Instead of accepting Jesus' offer of the kingdom, the Jews rejected him. Here is what Ice says:

"I believe the scriptures teach that Israel could have obtained her much sought after messianic kingdom by recognizing Jesus as the Messiah. We all know the sad reality–the Jews rejected Jesus. As a result the kingdom is no longer near but postponed, awaiting Jewish belief, which will occur at the end of the Tribulation."[44]

So, because the Jews rejected Jesus, the countdown of the 70 Weeks of Daniel 9 was suspended, or postponed, until the time comes when the Jews will accept Jesus, and the kingdom will be established. Jack Van Impe says that when Jesus died, "At that very moment, the prophetic clock stopped as far as Daniel's vision is concerned, and 40 years later the Jews were dispossessed of their country and scattered throughout the world."[45]

This suspension of the 70 Week prophetic countdown is 100% critical to the dispensational view. As we noted above, Ice, a leading millennialist, says that if there is no 2000 years gap between the 69ᵗʰ and 70ᵗʰ week of Daniel, then, "The dispensational system falls apart."

Let's take a closer look at Daniel. We are not going to get into the mathematical calculations of the 70 Weeks and where to start the count of the Weeks. We are not even going to get into a discussion of the ending point of the Weeks. See my book *Seal Up Vision and Prophecy* for that discussion. Instead, we are going to approach this discussion in a manner that we have not seen developed by any other commentator, and yet, it seems to me that it is the simplest way to deal with the issue.

It is my basic assumption that Jesus knew the prophecy of Daniel 9 better than anyone, since, after all, it was the spirit of Christ that prompted the Old Testament prophets to speak and write (1 Peter 1:11-12; 2 Peter 1:19f). Wouldn't you agree that Jesus would know Daniel's prophecy better than anyone else? Wouldn't you agree that he knew more about it than any of today's prophecy prognosticators? This seems so self evident as to be beyond dispute.

A second point that needs to be clarified is that there is virtual agreement that at the end of the 70 Weeks, the kingdom of God would be established. In a radio debate with Ice, I asked him if he would agree that this is true, and he agreed. So, at the end of the 70 Weeks, the kingdom of God was to be established. This would be the bringing in of everlasting righteousness. The kingdom would be the climax of the 70 Weeks.

With that in mind, take a look at the words of John the Baptizer: "Repent for the kingdom of heaven is at hand" (literally, "has drawn near," Matthew 3:2). In Mark 1:15, Jesus echoed those words, "The time is fulfilled, the kingdom of God is at hand" (again, "has drawn near").

When Jesus said, "The time is fulfilled," this refers to the prophecy of Daniel. So, Jesus, who knew Daniel 9 better than anyone, said the kingdom was near. However, the kingdom was to be established *at the end of the 70 Weeks* of Daniel 9. Therefore, the end of the 70 Weeks of Daniel 9 was near.

If the kingdom was not near, Jesus should not have said it was. But if he did know Daniel, and of course he did, then *he was speaking the truth* when he said the kingdom had drawn near. But again, this can only mean one thing, and that is that the end of the 70 Weeks was not far off.

This is where the millennialists come up with the gap theory. Ice says there is actually a gap, of so far 2000 years, *in the text of Daniel 9*. Well if this is true, consider the following.

If there is a gap: Jesus either *did or did not know* about it.

If there is a gap, of 2000 years, in Daniel 9, and, if Jesus knew of it, then when he announced the nearness of the kingdom, (i.e. the end of the 70th week), he was *purposely giving the wrong impression* to his audience, or, he did not know how long the gap was to be.

If there is a gap in Daniel 9, and Jesus knew, but *did not know* how long it was supposed to be, *his knowledge of Daniel's prophecy is impugned.* Yet, for Jesus to say that the end of the 70th week was near, demands that he thought he knew what Daniel actually predicted. If he thought he knew, but didn't, clearly, this impugns his Deity. Jesus clearly claimed to know what time it was.

If there is a gap in Daniel 9, and *Jesus knew* of it, he should have known that he could not even *truthfully* offer the kingdom to Israel. If there is a gap of 2000 years, and Jesus knew of it, then he had to know that the kingdom was *not near*, and he could not truthfully offer Israel the fulfillment of her hope.

If there is a gap in Daniel 9, then, even if Jesus did ostensibly offer the kingdom, *Israel could not accept that offer*, because the prophecy of the kingdom was not truly for Jesus' generation.

On the other hand, if *there is no gap*, of 2000 yrs, *in the text* of Daniel 9:24-27, and, Jesus said the kingdom, which is to come *at the end of the 70ᵗʰ week*, was at hand, then *Jesus was right* to say the kingdom, for the end of the 70ᵗʰ week, was near.

If there is no gap in the text of Daniel 9, but, the kingdom was postponed due to Jewish rebellion, then it must be true that the Lord *created a gap* between the 69ᵗʰ and 70ᵗʰ, that was *not originally in the text* of Daniel 9. This means that Daniel's original prediction *failed*. This also means Jesus failed, in his prediction of the nearness of the kingdom. This means that God failed, since He supposedly sent his Son "at just the right time" to fulfill Daniel's prophecy.

If there is no gap, and, if Jesus would have established the kingdom, (Ice *Tribulation,* 115), had not the Jews rejected him, this means that *Jesus was right* to say the kingdom, and thus the end of the 70ᵗʰ week, was at hand. But if there is no gap, and Jesus was right to say the kingdom was near, then if God did not establish the kingdom as Jesus promised, then Daniel's prophecy failed. Jesus failed. God failed.

It should be clear from this evidence that the millennial view of things is distorted to say the least. The idea of a gap in the text of Daniel 9 is simply without any Biblical merit at all. It violates Jesus' statements in the New Testament. Daniel 9 does predict the time of the end. That much is certain. And what is also certain is that Jesus, by saying that the establishment of the kingdom was near, believed and taught that the time of the end, the end of the 70 Weeks, was near. This brings us to another major prophecy of the time of the end.

DANIEL 12

There is no question that Daniel 12[46] predicts the time of the end, because the time of the end is mentioned at least three times in the text (v. 4, 9,13). We need to take quick note of several things.

First, as just noted, the prophecy is about the last days. Please take special note however, that it is *not* about the "end of time." There is a huge difference between the "time of the end" and the "end of time." These are *not* synonymous terms.

Second, Daniel was *not* living in the time of the end. He was told to, "seal the book until the time of the end" (v. 4). The book would remain, "sealed until the time of the end" (v. 9).

Third, Daniel's prophecy is about *the end of Israel's history*, not the end of human history. And, this is good news! Notice that the vision is given to Daniel and is, like Daniel 9, concerned with *Daniel's people* (v. 1), and that is Israel. Notice that the vision would be fulfilled, "when the power of the holy people is completely shattered" (v. 7). This is critically important. Daniel was told that the time of the end would be when the power of the holy people was completely shattered.

Who were Daniel's "holy people?" It can't be the church, because according to Daniel's other prophecies, the church will never be destroyed (Daniel 2:44; 7:13-14). However, here in chapter 12, the power of *some* holy people was destined to perish completely.

Thus, we have another passage that deals with the time of the end. It is about the last days of Israel, not about the end of time.

When was the power of the holy people completely shattered? That is easy for anyone with a knowledge of history. In A.D. 70, when the Romans conquered Israel. Jerusalem and the Temple, the center of Jewish life, was destroyed. The Temple was the heart and the core of Israel. To destroy the Temple was to destroy the nation.

At the same time, the genealogies were destroyed. This meant that the only way to confirm the identity of true priests was now lost forever. In addition, the tablets of the Torah were destroyed. The sacrifices were removed. Jerusalem, "the perfection of beauty" (Psalms 50:1f) was destroyed, not so much by the Romans as by Israel herself, and of course, ultimately by Jesus.

Daniel 12 is important, because, as we shall see, it is the source for Jesus' doctrine of the time of the end. Now, if we know that Daniel's prediction of the time of the end was concerned with the last days of Israel, then since Jesus based his doctrine of the end on Daniel, that means that Jesus' doctrine of the time of the end was about the last days of Israel.

What we have seen in Daniel then, is perfectly consistent with everything we have seen to this point. Daniel predicted events for the last days, but confined his prophecy to the days of the Roman Empire, and more specifically, he confined his predictions of the time of the end to a discussion of the end of Israel's distinctive relationship with God. Daniel does not speak about the time of a Revived Roman Empire, but the Roman Empire of the first century. Just like Genesis, Deuteronomy and Isaiah, in Daniel, the last days are confined to the first century, and of course, to the promises made to Israel.

In chapter 12 of his vision, Daniel was given some specific instructions. He was told to, "seal the book until the time of the end" and, "the words are closed up and sealed till the time of the end." (Daniel 12:4,

10). This is very plain. Daniel was told that his vision of the last days was *not near*. He was going to die. The events were not for his generation.

However, when we come to the book of Revelation we find something remarkable about Daniel's sealed book. We find Jesus opening the book! Here is why this is so important. Daniel was told that his book was to be sealed, "until the time of the end." (Daniel 12:10), and John saw Jesus opening the sealed book, containing Daniel's vision (Revelation 5). *John was living in the time of the end foretold by Daniel.*

John did not see a vision of Jesus opening the sealed book in the far off future, after the passing of 2000 years. John was told, "The time is at hand," and, "these things must shortly come to pass." The contrast between Daniel and Revelation in regards to the arrival of the time of the end is proof positive that John was indeed living in the last days, and this means of course, that if John was living in the last days, the time of the end foretold by Daniel, that all attempts to apply Daniel's prophecies to events 2000 years removed from John are misguided to say the least.

Note finally one of the most powerful contrasts in the scriptures. It must be remembered and emphasized that Daniel was told to seal his vision because its fulfillment was so far in the distant future that he was going to die before its fulfillment. However, in Revelation 22:10, John was told: "Do not seal the words of the prophecy, for the time is at hand."

It was about 500 years from Daniel until the time of John, and Daniel was told to *seal his vision* because it would not be fulfilled for a long time. Its fulfillment was *not at hand*. However, it has now been *four times longer* from John to the present than it was from Daniel to John, yet, we are supposed to believe that Revelation has not been fulfilled! We are supposed to believe that just because God told John the fulfillment was "at hand" that this does not mean anything. Well, if "at hand" wasn't supposed to mean anything to John, did, "Seal the book until the time of the end, for it shall be for many days," mean anything to Daniel? Did *"not at hand"* mean *anything*?

This contrast between the temporal standing of Daniel and John cannot be ignored. The expressions of a long time versus at hand must be honored. When we honor this language, it means that John was living in the time of the end 2000 years ago. Not only was John living in the last days, but, when we honor the frame-work of the last days as established in Daniel, we see that John was living *in the last days of Israel.*

We must emphasize that Daniel was told to seal the book because the last days events were not for his generation. He was going to die before they were fulfilled. However, John was told *not to seal* the book because the events were so near. This indicates that the fulfillment of the last days prophecies of Daniel was to occur in John's generation, perhaps even while John was alive. Why would Daniel be told to seal the book because it was *not for his lifetime*, but John be told not to seal the book because the fulfillment was so near, if the events were not for John's generation?

Daniel did not believe he was living in the time of the end. He did not believe that he was living in the last days. However, John did believe that *he* was living in the time of the end foretold by Daniel, and that the end was so near that he could not even seal the book of his prophecy. This means it is wrong for Bible students to take what John wrote and apply it to events two millennia removed from John's generation.

WHAT ABOUT THE END OF THE WORLD?

At this point, someone might say, "Well, okay, I can see that the passages you have cited do apply to the end of the Old World of Israel, but the Bible does predict the end of the world."

One of, if not the key, passage that most people point to as proof for the "end of the world" is Matthew 24:3: "And as He sat upon The Mount of Olives, the disciples came unto him privately, saying, 'Tell us, when shall these things be, and what shall be the sign of thy coming and of the end of the world?'" (KJV).

Here is the problem. When the disciples asked about the "end of the world" (King James), they were not asking about the end of time, or the end of the material world at all. The problem lies in the mistranslation of the word *aion*, (#165 in *Strong's Exhaustive Concordance)*. Properly translated it means *end of the age*, not end of the world. The proper translation gives a different understanding of the passage. This correction has been made in the *New King James* translation as well as most other modern translations.

When the disciples asked about the "end of the age" they used a distinctive Greek term *suntelia ton aionion*. This term is used very few times in the New Testament, and in each case it refers to the end of the Old Covenant Age. Let's take a look at those passages.

MATTHEW 13:39F

The correct use of words in their proper place is necessary to convey the true picture of God's Holy inspired message. That is why scripture, and scripture alone, has to be our final authority. In Matthew 13:39f, Jesus spoke of the time of the harvest, the time of the establishment of the kingdom: "The harvest is at the end of the age, (*suntelia aionos)* and the reapers are the angels." In verse 40 Jesus said: "As the tares are gathered and burned in the fire, so shall it be at the end of this age." *(sunteleia tou aionos)* In verse 49 he used the same term again. So, in one passage this distinctive term is used three times, more than in any other passage. What can we discover from the usage in Matthew 13? Plenty!

First, please notice that Jesus said that harvest is at the end of "this age." One of the most critical elements of proper interpretation is to ask "when." When was a statement made? When does the speaker/writer speak or write about. These are vital questions that seem to escape the majority of modern Bible students when they read these verses.

So, here is our question: In what age was Jesus living when he said, "harvest is at the end of 'this age'"? Was Jesus living in the Christian Age? Clearly not! Was he living under the Old Covenant Age of Moses? Yes, indeed, for we know that Christ appeared, "In the fulness of time, born of a woman, made under the Law" (Galatians 4:4). Thus, when Jesus said that the kingdom would come at the end of "this age" he was saying that the kingdom would arrive at the end of the Mosaic Age.

Second, this is directly confirmed by the fact that in verse 43, Jesus said, "Then shall the righteous shine forth as the sun in the kingdom of their Father," Jesus was citing Daniel 12:3. Why is this so important?

It is important because, as we have seen in our study of Daniel, Daniel foretold the "time of the end"[47] (Daniel 12:4). Furthermore, and this is what is so critical, Daniel was told that the fulfillment of his prophecy would be, "when the power of the holy people has been completely shattered" So, Jesus, anticipating the arrival of the kingdom, and living under the Mosaic Age, said, "Harvest shall be at the end of this age," The arrival of the kingdom would be when Daniel 12:3 was fulfilled. However, Daniel says that the end of the age would arrive *when Israel was completely destroyed.* The harmony here is precise. The time of the end is placed by both Daniel and Jesus as the end of the Old Covenant World of Israel. It has nothing to do with the end of the Christian Age.

MATTHEW 24:3

The next time the term "end of the world" is used in the Bible, using that distinctive Greek term *suntelia ton aionion*, is in the famous passage of Matthew 24. Jesus had just castigated the nation of Israel for her long history of persecuting the righteous saints, and said that judgment was coming on her in that generation.

As Jesus and his disciples left the Temple, the disciples began pointing out to him the stones of that magnificent edifice. And little wonder they should do so. That building complex was considered one of the wonders of the ancient world. The architectural stones used to construct it were the largest of any building ever found regardless of location. That place was huge and beautiful!

Jesus continued his condemnation of that wonderful building, "Do you not see all of these things? Assuredly I say to you, not one stone shall be left standing here upon another" (Matthew 24:2). In response to this prediction, the disciples immediately asked, "Tell us, when shall these things be, and what shall be the sign of your coming and the end of the age? (*suntelias tou aionos*). It is common for commentators to say that the disciples could not imagine the destruction of the Temple without thinking of the destruction of the material world at the same time. Even John Calvin said that the disciples, "Did not suppose that while the building of this world stood, the temple could fall to ruins."[48] This is clearly false. Were the disciples not aware that the Temple had been destroyed by the

Babylonians in B. C. 586? Surely! Did the literal world end at that time? Hardly. Well, if the disciples knew that the Temple had been destroyed in B. C. 586, and that the literal world was not destroyed then, what makes us think they were thinking of *the end of time* when Jesus predicted the destruction of the Temple for his generation?[49]

It is critical to think like the disciples thought, and to honor the basic rules of hermeneutic. Now, *hermeneutic* is a fancy word for the rules of interpretation. You and I honor those rules every time we read a newspaper, a novel, or even text books. Those rules say that when you are reading a text of any kind that you ask *Who?, What?, When?, Where?, Why? and How?*. It is improper to take a text, regardless of what it is, and divorce it from the time it was written, or what it was written about, and apply it to a time far removed. For instance, if you were to be rummaging through love letters from your grandfather, written to your grandmother when the two of them were dating, and in one of the letters granddad had written and said, "I am going to come visit you real soon!", would it be appropriate to begin telling everyone, "Grandpa is coming real soon!"'?

This is the problem we confront when we approach the disciples' questions. They asked Jesus about *the end of the age*. But what happens is that modern readers divorce the disciples from the age in which they were living, and put them down in the 21st century, and have them asking about the end of the Christian Age, or the end of time! *This is not good!*

The Temple did not represent the Christian Age, and it did not represent the existence of *time,* per se. It represented the Mosaic Age. The disciples were asking about the end of the Age that the Temple symbolized!

Ask yourself this question: *What age did the Temple represent?* Did the Temple represent the Christian Age? Not at all! Did it represent the time/space continuum, per se? No. Well, if the Temple did not represent physical creation, and if it did not symbolize the Christian Age, what makes us think that Jesus' prediction of the destruction of the Temple caused the disciples to think of the end of time, or the end of the Christian Age? Logically, would they not associate the destruction of the Temple with the end of the Age that the Temple symbolized?

It will be helpful to remind ourselves of some important facts.

First, The Jews believed in only two ages, what they called "this age" and, "the age to come."[50] Jesus and the New Testament writers concurred in that doctrine.

Second, the Jews believed that "this age" was *the age of Moses and the Law*. The "age to come" was the age of Messiah and the New Covenant.

Third, the age of Moses and the Law was to end. The age of Messiah and the New Covenant was to be eternal.

With this in mind, and reminding ourselves again of what age the Temple represented, it should be clear that Jesus' prediction about the destruction of the Temple was not a prediction of the end of time, and it was not a prediction of the end of the Christian Age. It was a prophecy of the end of the Age of Moses and the Law. Furthermore, *the disciples were not confused or mistaken* about what Jesus was predicting, or what they were asking about. They were inquiring about the end of the age that the Temple represented.

This fits perfectly what we have seen in Matthew 13. If you will remember, we saw that Jesus, in predicting the end of the age, said that it would be when Daniel 12:3 was fulfilled. But Daniel 12:3 would be fulfilled when the power of the holy people was completely shattered (Daniel 12:7). By the way, it is important to realize that in Matthew 13, when Jesus taught his disciples about the end of the age, he asked if they understood, and they said, "Yes" (Matthew 13:51)![51]

Jesus said that the end of the age would be when Daniel's prediction of the destruction of Israel was fulfilled. The disciples said they understood this. How then do we claim that when Jesus predicted the destruction of the Temple (the symbol of Israel's power!), that all of a sudden they forgot what Jesus had said earlier? At what point did the disciples forget Jesus' application of Daniel's prophecy concerning the end of the age when Israel was destroyed, and make the leap to thinking about the end of an age totally unrelated to Israel? Why would they think that the destruction of the Temple would be in any way linked with the destruction of the Age of Messiah, when everything they had ever been taught about the Age of Messiah said it was to be an *unending Age?*

Before we end this section we have to comment on the significance of the issue before us. The millennialists insist the disciples were mistaken to associate the Temple's demise with the end of the age. So, Jesus discussed the end of the age in Matthew 24, and ignored the discussion of the Temple's demise until he finally got around to saying a few words about it in Luke 21:20-24.

However, by understanding that *the disciples were not wrong* to associate the fall of Jerusalem with the end of the age, and realizing that the

Temple was destroyed in that generation, we can know that the end of the age came in that generation. This simple, yet profound understanding undermines the millennial madness of our times. The argument is simple: The destruction of the Temple (the one standing when the disciples asked their question.), was the end of the age. But the destruction of the Temple (the one standing when the disciples asked their question), occurred in Jesus' generation. Therefore, the end of the age occurred in Jesus generation at the destruction of the Temple (the one standing when the disciples asked their question).

There is absolutely no justification for divorcing the destruction of the Temple (the one standing when the disciples asked their question), from the discussion of the end of the age. That is the association the disciples made, and it is the association that Daniel and Jesus made. Unless one can show that the Temple represented a *different age*, and that the disciples had good reason for linking Jesus' prediction of the demise of the Temple (the one standing then), with the end of that *other age*, then we must, no matter how unsettling to traditional beliefs, acknowledge that the end of the age on the mind of the disciples was the end of the age represented by the Temple, and that was the age of Moses and the Law.

So, as we continue our study of the distinctive Greek term *suntelia ton aionon*, end of the age, what we have seen thus far forbids us from applying that term to the end of the Christian Age. It applies to the end of the Old Covenant Age of Israel that occurred with the fall of Jerusalem in A.D. 70. We go now to another text where this important term is used.

MATTHEW 28:18-20

As Jesus prepared to ascend back to the Father, he gave his disciples some final instructions and promises:

"Go therefore and make disciples of all the nations, baptizing them in the name of the Father and of the Son, and of the Holy Spirit, teaching them to observe all things that I have commanded you; and lo, I am with you always, even to the end of the age."

We are told that this passage has to refer to the end of the Christian Age, because if it doesn't, then Jesus is not with the church. He promised to be with his disciples, did he not? And did he not promise to be with them to the end of the age? So, to say that the end of the age has come is to say that Christ is no longer with the church, right? Wrong! Let's look closer.

First, Jesus is using the identical Greek term here that he used in Matthew 13 and Matthew 24. We have shown that those passages cannot refer to some future end of the Christian Age, but to the end of the Mosaic Age. Thus, the principle of consistency suggests that unless we can prove beyond doubt, from the text, that Jesus is using the term in a totally different way than before, we must define it the same way here.

Second, there is every reason to believe that Jesus was promising that he would be with the disciples *miraculously* until the end of the age. After all, the consistent Biblical doctrine is that the miraculous gifts would continue until the end of the age (Acts 2:16f; 1 Corinthians 1:4-8; 1 Corinthians 13:8f, etc.). Space forbids development of this idea here. See my other works for a full discussion of this passage. Suffice it to say that the charismata ceased at the end of the Jewish Age in AD 70.

Third, and this is critical, Jesus said the gospel was to go into all the world before the end of the age. This allows us to positively identify the end of the age Jesus had in mind. Let's go to Matthew 24. Remember that the disciples asked Jesus for a sign of the end of the age (Matthew 24:3). One of the key signs that Jesus gave was, "This gospel of the kingdom will be preached in all the world as a witness to all the nations, and then the end will come." The completion of the World Mission would be a sign of the end of the age. We have shown that this is a referent to the Old Covenant Age. Was the gospel preached into all the world in that generation? Yes!

Our millennial friends claim that the gospel has never been preached into all the world, but is being proclaimed today as never before. The trouble is, this denies the plain statements of the Bible. The Bible affirms in the clearest terms possible that the gospel had been preached into all the world before the fall of Jerusalem. To illustrate this, the next chart (revised and edited), is from my book *Into All The World, Then Comes the End.* That book is an in-depth study of the question of the World Mission and the end of the age. For our purposes here, I just want to note the fact that when Jesus predicted and commanded the World Mission, that he used several Greek words, translated *world, earth, creation,* etc.. Then, the New Testament writers, *inspired by the Holy Spirit,* used those *identical words* to say that the gospel had been preached in all the world! This is more than a little impressive. Take a look at the chart.

Jesus' Command or Prophecy	Paul's Inspired Statements
Gospel shall be preached in all the world (Greek, *oikoumene*) Matthew 24:14	Gospel *has been preached* into all the world (Greek, *oikoumene*) Romans 10:18 (circa 57 A.D.)
For a witness to *all the nations* (Greek, *pasin tois ethnesin*) Matthew 24:14; 28:19	Gospel is made manifest "to all the nations" (Greek, *panta ta ethne*) Romans 16:26 (circa 62 AD)
Go into all the *world* (Greek, *kosmos*) Mark 16:15	Gospel has been preached into all the world (Greek, *kosmos*) Colossians 1:6
Preach to every *creature* (Greek, *ktisis*)	Gospel has been preached to every creature (Greek, *ktisis*) Colossians 1:23
Preach to Judea, Samaria, uttermost parts of the world (Greek, *ge*)	Gospel has been preached into all the earth (Greek, *ge*) Romans 10:18

You will notice that *every Greek word* used by Jesus to predict or to command the preaching of the gospel into all the world is used by Paul, inspired by the Spirit, to say the gospel *had been preached to that very extent.* Yet, most people today deny that the gospel was preached into all the world. They say, "Are you telling me that the gospel was preached to South America? Are you saying it was preached to Russia?"

Ice refuses to accept the inspired testimony of Paul:

"The two references in Colossians (Colossians 1:6, 1:23, dkp) are used in a similar way, saying, in essence that Christ's Great Commission (Matthew 28:18-20; Mark 16:16; Luke 24) was making progress, even in the first century. This is clear from the fact that Paul uses the Greek preposition "in, *en*" in all three passages (Romans 1:8; Colossians 1:6, 23), as a *dative of sphere*, telling us, "the sphere or realm in which the world to which it is related takes place or exists." This means that the three Pauline statements tell the reader that the gospel is spreading in or throughout the sphere of the whole world. These passages do not tell us that this process is complete and preparing the way for the AD 70 judgment, as preterists would have us to believe. Instead, we learn that the evangelization of the world has only just begun in the first century, and is making great progress."(*Tribulation*, 134).

Here is the problem for Ice. He says, "Has been preached into all the world," means, "has begun to be preached." However, that is a distortion of the text. Paul had lots of Greek words available to him that would say the Gospel had *begun* to be preached, and he did not use them. He said the Gospel had been preached.

Furthermore, Ice's claim that the *dative of sphere* limits the scope of the preaching is a misuse of the Greek, and ignores the facts. Jesus said the Gospel was to be preached *into all the world*. He used the Greek term (*eis panta ta ethna*), *with the dative of sphere*. Paul said the Gospel had been preached *into all the world*, and he used the identical Greek term (*eis panta ta ethne, Romans 16:26*), that Jesus did in Mark 13:10. Now, if Jesus used the dative of sphere, and Paul used the identical words *with the dative of sphere*, only a preconceived idea would say that Paul was saying something totally different than Jesus.

Ice continues his denial of the fulfillment of the World Mission in *End Times Controversy*. Commenting on Colossians 1, he says that all Paul meant when he said the gospel had been preached into all the world was, "Paul was saying that the gospel has come, or been introduced to the Colossian believers, just as it had come, or been introduced, in all the world. So this is not a statement about whether the gospel has been preached to a certain area per se; rather it is a statement about the arrival of the gospel as a global message." (P. 174)

The problem for Ice is that Paul said the world had heard the gospel and responded to it in the same way as at Colossae. And notice that Paul was definitely saying that the gospel had been preached to a certain area. It had been *preached* in the "certain area" of Colossae, had it not?

So, here is the question: was the gospel actually preached to the Colossians? Did the Colossians *actually hear* the gospel proclaimed, and did they actually respond to that message? Or was the gospel simply introduced into town, but no one heard it? If the Colossians actually *heard* the gospel, and if the Colossians actually *responded* to the gospel message, then the gospel had been *preached* and *responded* to in the *world* in the same way! So, if the gospel had not actually been preached in all the world, then the gospel had not actually been preached at Colossae! Whatever happened in reality at Colossae had happened in reality in the world.

Here is our point: what ever Jesus meant by the word *world* when he commanded and predicted the World Mission, the Holy Spirit gave Paul *the identical words* when he said the gospel *had been preached into all the world.* Did the Spirit put a different meaning on the identical words without indicating that there was a difference? If Paul had wanted to say that the gospel had been preached into all the world, would not his statement that the gospel "has been preached to every creature under heaven" not convey that message? What is there about "has been preached to all the nations" that says, "It has *not* been preached to all the nations"? How is it possible to turn *"has been"* into *"has not been"?*

If you want to define the "world" in Paul as a different world than that intended by Jesus, you must be able to show the difference in the words. You cannot simply affirm, "Well, Paul had a different view of the world than we did." You cannot simply *say*, "Jesus meant the world as we know it, but Paul meant *his* world." You must *prove from the text* that there is a different definition for "world" in Matthew than that in Romans. You must *prove* that the identical words are being used in radically different ways, even though the topic is the same, and even though it was the same Spirit that was inspiring the declarations.

What makes this impossible is this: Jesus told his disciples that the gospel was to be preached into all the world, then the end would come. In other words, the completion of the World Mission was to be a sign of the nearness of the end of the age. He told them that when they saw the signs being fulfilled, they could know the end was near (Matthew 24:32). Here is a question to ponder: when Paul said the gospel had been preached into all the world, did he also then proclaim that the end was near? Yes, he did!

In Romans 16 Paul said the gospel had been preached to all the nations. In chapter 13:11f he said, "The night is far spent, the Day is at hand." In chapter 16:20, he said, "The God of peace shall crush Satan under your feet shortly!" So, Jesus gave the completion of the world mission as a sign of the end of the age. Paul said the gospel had been preached into all the world, and then says the end was near.

What we have in Matthew 28 then is this: Jesus not only used the identical term (end of the age), that has been proven to refer to the end of the Jewish Age, but, his command of the World Mission in relation to the end of the age, when compared with his discourse in Matthew 24, demands that the end of the age in Matthew 28 is the same end of the age as in Matthew 24. This means that the end of the age in Matthew 28 is the Old Covenant Age of Israel. Let's turn now to examine the last of the verses where the distinctive term end of the age (*sunteliea ton aionion*) is used.

"He then would have had to suffer often since the foundation of the world; but now, once at the end of the ages, He has appeared to put away sin by the sacrifice of Himself."

This passage is the final time that the distinctive Greek term *sunteliea ton aionon* appears in scripture. We have seen that in each of the preceding passages that this term refers not to the end of the Christian Age, but to the end of the Old Covenant World of Israel. The principle of consistency would indicate that this is its meaning here, and the text confirms that thought. Let's take a closer look.

First, it says that Jesus appeared in the end of the age.

Second, it specifies for us what he came to do in the end of the age, offer his life as an atoning sacrifice.

Third, this specificity identifies the age in which he appeared, because it is clear that Jesus did not appear in the end of the Christian Age, and he most assuredly did not appear in the end of time!

Fourth, the Bible is plain about when Jesus appeared: "In the fulness of time, God sent forth His Son, made of a woman *born under the law*, to redeem them that were under the Law" (Galatians 4:4-5, my emphasis).

Now, since Jesus was born under the Law, and died to deliver those under the Law, and he gave his life in *the end of the age*,[52] does it not follow inexorably, that the end of the age reference is to the end of the Old Covenant World of Moses and the Law? Unless a person is willing to say that Jesus' death occurred at the end of the Christian Age, or that the Hebrew writer mistakenly believed that Jesus' appearance was to bring the literal time-space continuum to an end, then the most logical thing to do is to identify *the end of the ages* as a referent to the end of the Mosaic Age.

SUMMARY OF THIS SECTION

So, what have we seen so far? We have examined every passage that specifically mentions the "end of the age" and we have seen that every occurrence of the distinctive term *sunteliea ton aionon* refers to the same thing, the end of the Old Age of Israel. And, since we have seen that the Bible teaches that the Christian Age has no end, this makes perfect sense. The *only age* that was to end was the Old Covenant Age. The fact is that the Bible no where uses the term "end of time," and no where uses the term "end of the Christian Age."

As a matter of fact, it would be good at this point to take note of what the Bible does say about the literal world, and its durability.

John Anderson notes that there are several passages in the Bible that teach that the earth is permanent. Psalms 78:69 states, "And he hath built his sanctuary like high palaces, like the earth which he has established forever" (Strongs #776). This verse states that the earth is established forever. Psalms 93:1, "The Lord reigneth, he is clothed with majesty, the Lord is clothed with strength, wherewith he hath girded: The world also is established that it cannot be moved." The word, *world*, here is # 8398 in Strong's Concordance and means, "the earth-the globe-the Land." Psalms 104:5. "Who laid the foundations of the earth, (Strong's #776) that it should not be removed forever?" The same word, *erets*, is used as in Psalm 78:69. Ecclesiastes 1:4. "One generation passeth away, and another generation cometh, but the earth (#776) abideth forever."[53]

Other passages could be cited, but these should be sufficient to make it plain that the Bible teaches that the earth is established forever and is without end.[54] That is good news!

The consistent story from the Old Testament to the New is that the Old Covenant World –the "heaven and earth" of Israel--had to end, in order to bring in the endless New World of the Messiah. The Old World was characterized by words like darkness, sin, and death. That is why those under that Old Age longed for "the age about to come." They knew that in the New Age of the Messiah, they could have eternal life, and fellowship with the Father in a way that could never be under the Old Law (see Hebrews 9:6-10). These are the blessings that are now a reality in Christ, because he did sweep away the Old World in the destruction of the Temple and Jerusalem in A.D. 70.

BUT WHAT ABOUT ALL THE SIGNS?

Those who say the end of the age is near insist that we see today the predicted signs of that event. Jack Van Impe claims that no other generation has ever seen so many signs fulfilled. LaHaye and Ice claim the same thing, going so far as to say that since World War I, there has been a "parade of signs" being fulfilled. Of course, this is just *another contradiction* in the millennial view of things. On the one hand Ice and LaHaye claim that since 1948 there has been a veritable "parade of signs," "in fulfillment of Matthew 24:8." On the other hand, Ice says, "Matthew 24:4-14 cannot happen until after the rapture and the start of the Tribulation." *(End Times,* 167). That is a major contradiction any way you look at it!

On a pre-recorded Trinity Broadcasting program, popular prophecy teacher John Hagee said the (then) current Iraqi crisis was the beginning of the end, and that the rapture would likely occur *within six months* (3-20-03). The host, Benny Hinn, appeared shocked, and asked "Are we that close? Are you saying the rapture could be in six months?" Hagee responded, "We are that close."

It seems not to have occurred to these prognosticators, that virtually every generation has claimed the identical thing. Martin Luther claimed that all of the signs necessary for the end had already been fulfilled, and they were just waiting for the end.

Jesus however, said that the signs of the end of the age, and the end itself, would occur in "this generation" (Matthew 24:34). That was *his* generation. Ice, in a radio debate with me, said that *none* of the signs given by Jesus in Matthew 24, were fulfilled in the first century generation, therefore the end of the age could not have occurred in that generation. However, this is simply false.

If every major sign of the end of the age did occur in Jesus' contemporary generation then this demands that Jesus' prediction of the end of the age occurred then, and it means without doubt that the term "this generation" cannot be applied to our generation or a future generation.

The fact is that *every major sign*--not to mention the "minor" non-signs of earthquake, famine, pestilence, etc-- that the Bible predicted to occur just prior to the end of the age *appeared in the first century.*[55] We are not going to chronicle the fulfillment of Jesus' prediction of the famines, earthquakes, etc. since Jesus himself said that these were *not* true signs of the end "the end is not yet" (Luke 21:9).[56]

Thus, while you will hear Van Impe, Jeffrey, Hagee, Lindsay and others using newspaper reports about famine, war, pestilence, etc. to prove we are in the last days, we should take Jesus at his word when he said these were *not signs that the end had drawn near.* As a matter of fact, Jesus said it would be the *false prophets* who would appeal to these "non-signs" to claim "the end has drawn nigh" (Luke 21:8), and urged his disciples not to believe them. You just have to catch the power of this problem for the millennial view.

In *Charting*, (36), Ice and LaHaye claim that since 1948, "many other signs have occurred in fulfillment of Matthew 24:8." What did Matthew 24:8 predict? It predicted the appearance of many false teachers, and, in Luke 21:8, which is the direct parallel passage. The false teachers would say, "The end has drawn near!"

Do you see the problem? Jesus said there would be many false teachers looking at the wars, famines, earthquakes, etc., and proclaiming that the end was near, when in fact, those events are not signs of the end, "the end is not immediately" (Luke 21:8). Ice and LaHaye claim that since 1917,[57] and 1948 there has been a "parade of signs" of the end, and they even say that the restoration of Israel in 1948 is the "Super Sign of the Last Days." They are constantly proclaiming "the end has drawn near!" Yet, the end has not come. Thus, *if the end is yet in the future*, then Ice and LaHaye have, by their own prognostications, become identified as some of those false teachers who said the end was near when it was not truly near!

The Bible does list several major signs of the last days, and as we just stated, each of these major signs occurred in the first century. Let's take a look at the major signs of the last days.

Sign #1-- *Elijah was to come* before the end of the age. (Malachi 4:5-6). When you read the millennial literature you will find that there is an *open denial* that Elijah came as predicted. However, Jesus said John the Immerser was the predicted Elijah (Matthew 11:11-15; 17:9-13). Jesus' challenge, "He who has ears to hear let him hear," in Matthew 11 was a challenge for the Jews of his day–and their modern counterparts–to open their eyes to the realities before them. Their preconceived ideas were blinding them to God's truth. They needed to have eyes and ears attuned to what God was doing, and Jesus said Elijah had come! Their eyes did not believe what they were seeing however, so they did not believe. But, their unbelief did not change the Truth that John was Elijah.

But John, as Elijah, appeared in *Jesus' generation*. This is a vitally important issue that is being virtually ignored in the literature. Now, if Elijah was to come in the last days, and Jesus said that John was the anticipated Elijah, shouldn't we take his word for it? What right does anyone today have to say that Jesus was wrong, and that John really was not Elijah, when Jesus said he was?

Sign #2– *The outpouring of the Holy Spirit* was to occur in the last days (Joel 2:28-32). As we have seen, this prophecy, and Peter's application of it, is devastating to the prophecy pundits. On Pentecost, the Spirit was poured out, and Peter said, "This is that which was spoken by the prophet Joel" (Acts 2:15f). The outpouring of the Spirit occurred in *Jesus' generation*. One of the greatest theological tragedies is the open refusal of the millennial world to accept the inspired statements of Peter that the last days foretold by Joel were present in the first century. Of course, to admit that truth is to abandon dispensationalism, but the call of Scripture is, "Buy the Truth and sell it not!"

It is important to recall how important this issue really is. Remember that the millennialists claim that the last days countdown of Israel (that's the 70 Weeks of Daniel 9 discussed earlier), were suspended when the Jews rejected Jesus in Matthew 12. So, the last days of Israel, the last days foretold by the Old Testament prophets, should not have been, could not have been, present on Pentecost. If in fact the last days foretold by any of the Old Testament prophets were present on Pentecost, the entire millennial house of cards comes tumbling down. It is that simple.

So, consider again what it meant for Peter to say, "This is that which was spoken by the prophet Joel!" We say again that you cannot make Peter's "this is that" mean, "this is *not* that!" Yet, that is precisely what the millennialists attempt to do. One of the key signs of the last days was the outpouring of the Spirit. That occurred on Pentecost in A.D. 33, and the inspired apostle said it was the fulfillment of the last days predictions. This means, without doubt, that the last days were present on Pentecost, and this means that *the last days are not present today*.

Sign #3– In Matthew 24:14 Jesus said, "*this gospel of the kingdom shall be preached in all the world*, then comes the end." As we have just seen, Paul affirms, repeatedly, that the gospel had been preached into all the world (Romans 16:25-26, Colossians 1:23). This happened in *Jesus' contemporary generation*.

Here is another example of the willingness of the millennialist to deny the emphatic inspired statements of the Spirit. In a radio debate with Ice, the topic was the *Great Commission: Fulfilled or Future*. In spite of the fact that I cited numerous passages from Paul, see my chart again, Ice simply affirmed that what those passages meant is that the gospel had *begun* to be preached, and that Paul did not intend to say that the Great Commission was fulfilled. Would you take the time to get your Bible out, and to read each of the passages from Paul that are in the chart? Paul did not say that the gospel had *begun* to be preached into all the world. Paul did not say that the gospel was being preached into some, or even most, of the world. He said the gospel had been preached into all the world, and he used the identical Greek words used by Jesus to describe the world, and the realm of the world into which the gospel was to be preached. Jesus commanded and predicted the preaching into all the world. Paul spoke in past tenses to say it had been done.

Thus, the Spirit declared, *several times,* that one of the pivotal signs of the presence of the last days and the impending end of the age, the fulfillment of the World Mission, was fulfilled in the first century. And not only did the Spirit declare that the World Mission had been completed, He said the end of the age was near.

Sign #4– Jesus said that when *the Abomination of Desolation* appeared his disciples were to flee from Judea because of the coming tribulation (Matthew 24:15f). Please take note that Jesus was speaking to *living breathing human beings* when he said, "When *you* see the Abomination of Desolation spoken of by Daniel the prophet, then let those who are in Judea flee." (My emphasis) Jesus was speaking to his personal disciples, not in some vague, abstract, sense.

Here is an amazing fact of history. Church historian Eusebius says the early church fled Judea in about AD 66:

> "The whole body, however, of the church at Jerusalem, having been commanded by divine revelation, given to men of approved piety there before the war, removed from the city and dwelt at a certain town beyond the Jordan, called Pella. Here those that believed in Christ, having removed from Jerusalem, as if holy men had entirely abandoned the royal city itself, and the whole land of Judea; the divine justice overtook them, totally destroying the entire generation of these evildoers from the earth."[58]

So, we have the historical record that what Jesus commanded to be done when the Abomination appeared was done, and we are specifically told that they did what they did because of his command given concerning the Abomination. The only conclusion to be drawn from this is that the disciples believed they were *seeing what Jesus had predicted,* therefore, *they were doing what he commanded.* The Abomination of Desolation occurred in *Jesus' contemporary generation. This means of course, that the last days were in that generation.*

Sign #5– *The Great Apostasy* would be another sign of the last days (2 Thessalonians 2:2f). In Matthew 24:9-12, Jesus said the love of the "majority" (NASV) of people would grow cold. He said it would be in his generation (v. 34).

The New Testament documents the reality of that apostasy (Galatians 1:6f). Paul marveled that the Galatian churches were going off into apostasy so quickly. He was not writing to just one church with local problems. He was addressing an entire region, and all of the churches in that region. All you have to do is read Corinthians to see how widespread the doctrinal, moral, and ethical apostasy really was. When you read Colossians, 2 Peter 2, Jude, and many of the other epistles, it is easy to see that the apostasy was indeed widespread, and even at an early stage. The apostasy was a very real problem in the first century.

Sign #6– *The Man of Sin* was a sign of the last days. What is so amazing is that Paul specifically says that Man of Sin was *already alive* in his generation (2 Thessalonians 2:5-8). And yet, Paul's statement is virtually ignored by modern day Bible students. Paul not only says that the man of sin was already alive when he wrote Thessalonians (circa 52 A.D.), he said that the one holding him back, the restrainer, was already holding him back (2 Thessalonians 2:6-7)! Not only was the man of sin alive, and the restrainer present, but Paul said that *the Thessalonians knew the restrainer!* Now, if the man of sin was already alive, and if the restrainer was already holding him back, how in the name of reason can we take seriously the claims of men like Hal Lindsay who totally ignore these facts and claim that the man of sin is, "alive somewhere in Europe"?[59] Did Mr. Lindsay not even *read* Thessalonians?

The Bible thus gave *six major signs* of the last days, and e*very one of those signs occurred in Jesus' contemporary generation!* Therefore, in spite of the claims of men like Ice and other leading dispensational millennialists, that none of the signs were fulfilled, we have seen, from the inspired scriptures, that every major sign of the last days was indeed present in the first century generation.

We need to take a moment to examine the presence of the signs in another light. Jesus gave the signs of the end of the age, and then gave two bits of information:

First, he told his disciples that some "Christian prophets" would proclaim, "the end has drawn near," but their message would be *premature*. The disciples were not to believe those who proclaimed the nearness of the end before it was actually near (Luke 21:8).

Second, he told the disciples concerning the signs and the consequent declaration of the nearness of the end, "When you see all these things, know that it is near, even at the door" (Matthew 24:32; Luke 21:31).

With these two facts in mind, let us focus on the first point. When Jesus' disciples asked him about the end of the age (Matthew 24:3), he began to explain the events that had to happen before that consummative event. However, he warned them that before the end, there would be false signs, and false prophets saying the end was near when it was not actually near: "Take heed that you not be deceived. For many will come in My name, saying, 'I am He,' and, 'The time has drawn near.' Therefore, do not go after them" (Luke 21:8).

Jesus then gave two events that would signal the nearness of the end, the fulfillment of the World Mission, and the appearance of the Abomination would signal that the end had drawn near.

This is *extremely* important. Jesus was speaking to living breathing human beings, and told them that *they* would see these events. He was not speaking abstractly. He told his disciples that *they* would experience false teachers saying the end was near, (or present!), when in fact it was not. And, we know that these things happened very early in the first century.

In 2 Thessalonians 2, Paul had to write to the church to warn them not to believe the Lord had already come![60] Jesus said false prophets would come saying the end had come, or had drawn near, before it was. Paul had to deal with *that very problem* at an early time (circa A.D. 49).

Jesus told his disciples that they would see the fulfillment of the Great Commission and the Abomination of Desolation, and when they did, they would know that the end truly had drawn near.

As we have shown, in Romans, (57-59 A.D.), Paul said the Gospel had been preached into all the world.[61] In Colossians 1:5-7, 23, Titus 2:11-13, etc. (60-62 A.D.), the apostle said the Gospel had been preached, "to every creature under heaven," "to all men," "all the world," etc. And Peter--the author of 2 Peter 3:8-- stated, "The end of all things has drawn near...the time has come for the judgment to begin" (1 Peter 4:7, 17).

This time line is critical. At an early time, false prophets appeared in fulfillment of Jesus predictions, saying the end had drawn near, or had come. The apostles, cognizant of Jesus' warnings, rejected those prophets, reminding the disciples of what had to happen before the end could come. Then, some 10 years later, with the fulfillment of the first of the two major signs given by Jesus, the inspired writers say that the end had drawn near.

Jesus had said, "When you see these things you will know it, (the end of the age, DKP), is at the door" (Matthew 24:33). John, living at the time when he witnessed the fulfillment and appearance of the signs, said, "It is the last hour!" (1 John 2:18).

Only Jesus' first century apostles were authorized to say when the end was near. Those before them who said it was near, were false. Those *after* them who *say* it is near are wrong. They are the only ones who could know, *and they said it was near in the first century!*

This divine time line teaches us some important lessons. It shows that it truly was Jesus' generation that was to see the signs. Jesus was not saying that the fulfillment of the World Mission, or the appearance of the Abomination, was to be centuries in the future.

This time line, coupled with the apostles' rejection of the message of those who said the end was already present, also shows that the events were fulfilled in the first century.

This time line, when related to the later epistles, *after the fulfillment of the first of the two major signs given by Jesus*, in which the inspired writers emphatically stated, "The end of all things has drawn near" (1 Peter 4:7), proves that their time statements must be taken literally. Jesus had told them they could tell when the end had *not drawn near*, and he had told them when they could tell *it had drawn near, and when they saw the signs occurring they said "the end has drawn near!"*

Here is the power of Jesus' warning in Luke 21:8. Where ever you place his warning chronologically, all those before that time who proclaimed the nearness of the end are declared by Jesus himself to be false prophets. Was Jesus speaking *to the modern church* when he said, "Do not be deceived, many will come saying, 'The end has drawn near'"? If he was, then all previous generations of believers who have declared so confidently that the end was near in their generation are judged as false teachers by Jesus. Do you realize what this means? It means that Jesus' own apostles are false prophets because they said, unambiguously, "in a very, very little while, (*Greek, hosan, hosan micron*), and he who is coming will come, and will not tarry" (Hebrews 10:37).

Let me reiterate this, according to Luke 21:8 no generation was to declare the nearness of the end except the one that saw the signs. All "prophecy experts" that declared, or declare, the nearness of the end before (or *after!*), it is actually near, were to be, or are to be rejected. If therefore, Luke 21:8 applies *to the current generation*, there is no escaping the fact that Jesus' own apostles are adjudged as false prophets. We either accept their declarations of the nearness of the end as the definitive, truthful, final word on the issue, or else call them liars.

Thus, when the Biblical writers, writing in light of Jesus' warnings, said that what he had foretold was fulfilled, and that the end had drawn near, we cannot stretch those statements two thousand years into the future. We cannot ignore their statements of "at hand." All statements that the end was near, made *before* the inspired writers said it was near, were false. All statements that the end *is near*, written or stated *after* the Biblical writers said it was near, are false statements. The only preachers, prophets or teachers who were *ever* given divine insight into the time of Jesus' return were Jesus' first century inspired disciples, and they said that the end had drawn near 2000 years ago! If their statements that the end was near were as wrong as those before them, *then they too were false teachers.*

This is particularly relevant when we consider one of the passages considered earlier, Joel 2-3. Remember that Joel foretold the last days, when the Spirit would be poured out before the end of the age (Joel 2:28-30). Remember too that Peter, in Acts 2, quoted Joel's prophecy and said, "This is that which was spoken by the prophet Joel" (Acts 2;15f). Now, we want to notice something else Joel said.

In chapter 3 verse 14, Joel said that the end of the age was near. Now, lots of folks like to argue that Joel was saying that the Day was near when he wrote. This is simply misguided. Joel was speaking of the last days, and saying that when the last days finally arrived, the end of the age would be near. We might call this *projected imminence,* for it means that the writer/prophet is projected into the last days, to see the events of the end, and says that when the predicted time arrived, the end would be near.

Note what this means in light of Luke 21:8, and the rest of the New Testament. Joel said that in the last days, the end of the age would be near. The New Testament writers affirm that the last days were present, *"This is that which was spoken by the prophet Joel!"*, and they affirm repeatedly that the end was coming, "in a very, very little while," that, "the end of all things has drawn near" (1 Peter 4:7), and that "the end of the ages has come upon us" (1 Corinthians 10:11).

Joel said when the last days arrived, the end would be near. The New Testament writers said they were in the last days foretold by Joel, and the end was near. Will we believe them, or the modern day "experts" who deny their words?

This is incredibly significant. Joel said when the last days arrived, the end would be near. The apostles said they were in the last days foretold by Joel, and the end was near. Jesus told his disciples not to say the end was near until they saw the signs of the end. The disciples saw the signs, and began to proclaim the nearness of the end. If the disciples were not in the last days foretold by Joel, then the end was not near, and they were false prophets, period. Since Jesus told his disciples not to believe the premature announcements of the end, and told them only to proclaim the end when the end was truly near, then it must be true that their declarations that the last days were present were true. But of course, if the last days foretold by Joel and the Old Testament prophets really were present after Pentecost, then the modern day claims that Israel's last days are still future are falsified. The entire millennial house comes crashing down.

Note again that in Luke 21:8, Jesus told his disciples that *fellow believers* would *prematurely* say the end had drawn near (Luke 21:8). He told his apostles to reject those false prophets. However, he gave them the signs by which *they* could know the end was near (Matthew 24:32-33). The disciples, upon seeing the fulfillment of the first of those signs began to declare that the end was near. However, modern commentators tell us that they could not actually declare that the end was near. This means that Jesus' apostles were just as guilty of false teaching concerning the time of the end as those who said it was near before they did!

What is the difference between the Christians, that Jesus called false teachers, who prematurely said the end was near, and the apostles, who heralded that *same message in the same generation*? If those *before* the Bible writers were wrong, because their predictions were false, then the NT writers were wrong *for the identical reason*! Was there no difference between the message of those *before* the disciples who said "the end has drawn near," and the message of *the apostles themselves* who said "the end has drawn near?" If Jesus was not speaking to *his first century apostles about their generation*, then their statements, that the end had drawn near, qualify *them* as the false teachers Jesus said must be rejected! If the predictions of those *before* the apostles, and those of the apostles failed, then the apostles do indeed stand as false teachers.

Jeffrey uses the long history of prophecy pundits' claims that the end was near to prove his theory of the imminent end. He cites a fourth century writer, Ephraem: "We ought to understand thoroughly therefore, my brothers what is imminent or overhanging. Already there have been hunger and plagues, violent movements of nations and signs, which have already been fulfilled, and there is not other which remains, except the advent of the wicked one in the completion of the Roman kingdom. Brothers, the end of the world is at hand, believe me because it is the very last time."[62] Ephraem sounds a lot like Hal Lindsay and Grant Jeffrey!

Jeffrey also quotes Martin Luther: "I am satisfied that the last day must be before the door; for the signs predicted by Christ and the Apostles Peter and Paul have now all been fulfilled, the trees put forth, the Scriptures are green and flourishing...We certainly have nothing now to wait for but the end of all things."[63] In other words, the fact that Martin Luther, and those before and after him, said that the end was near, supposedly proves the end is near *today*.

Jeffrey spends considerable time documenting from patristic writings that the early church, from the second century onward, believed that the end was near (2001, 56f). He also lays stress on the fact that the apostles also believed in the nearness of the end. Thus, for Jeffrey, the modern church is justified in believing in the soon coming end because the apostles believed the end was near, and those who followed them believed the end was near. In other words, believers today are to look back upon this *history of failed predictions,* and be confirmed in the faith that the end is coming, and soon! However, Luke 21 refutes such an idea.

Jesus told his disciples that other believers would come, *before them,* falsely saying that the end was near, and that they, his disciples listening to him that day, could know when the end had truly drawn near. The apostles therefore, stand as *divinely and exclusively qualified* to be the true proclaimers of when the end was near. They were to reject as *false teachers* those who came before them saying the end was near.

If the apostles' declarations were no more true than those who pontificated before them, or no more true than Ephraem, than Luther, than William Miller, etc., then *their inspiration means nothing at all.* According to Jeffrey, MacArthur, Lindsay, et. al, those *before* the apostles, the apostles, and all prophecy pundits *after* the apostles stand together. But, if they all stand together, *then they all fall together,* for the predictions of those before the apostles, the apostles, and all those after the apostles have failed, if taken to refer to a literal physical return of Christ!

We must ask, did the *inspiration* of the apostles not set their predictions apart from those before or after them? Were the apostles not better qualified as discerners of the signs than those before, or after them? If not, in what way did the apostles differ from those whom Jesus *told them to avoid,* those proclaiming the end was near?

One thing is for sure, Jeffrey, Lindsay, Impe, MacArthur, etc. are no better at discerning the signs of the time than were the Montanists (2nd century), who insisted that all of the signs were fulfilled. No better than Ephraem of the fourth century, They are no better than the extremists of the eleventh century who insisted that all the signs were fulfilled as never before. They are no better than Martin Luther who said all the signs were fulfilled in the sixteenth century. They are no better than the Millerites/Adventists of the 19th century who carefully calculated the signs of the times, but failed. And, they are no better than the Jehovah's Witnesses of the 19-20th century who proclaimed that *without fail* all of the signs were fulfilled, and that the Lord would positively come in 1874, (changed then to) 1914, (then changed to) 1925, (changed once again to) 1975, etc.. Jeffrey is no different than all of these, for he says, just as they did, "No other generation has ever witnessed so many prophecies fulfilled in its lifetime as we have witnessed" (*Return*, 184). Must we, indeed, take a view that says the *apostles* were guilty of such error?

Finally, the time line of Luke 21:8 destroys the commonly stated view that God caused the apostles to make all of the emphatic time statements about the nearness of the end in order to keep the church of each successive generation "on the tiptoe of expectation." It also disproves the interpretation of Matthew 24:34, that Jesus did not mean *his generation* would see the end of the age, but instead, meant that the generation to see the signs would be the final generation, and that, when the signs would appear, believers could finally know that the end was truly near.

These views are wrong because Jesus condemned the pronouncement of the nearness of the end *before it was actually near!* Since the *apostles* did declare that the end was near in their generation, if the end was not truly near, then the NT writers are the very false teachers that Jesus warned about! He said many would come saying, "The end has drawn near," but condemned that premature message. In other words, *the church throughout countless generations is not to have the continual message that the end is near!* The *only generation* that was to proclaim the message of the soon coming end was to be the generation that would see the signs. Believers were to reject any message of the imminent end that was not the inspired word of the apostles. To suggest that God gave all of the NT statements that the end was near to create a sense of urgency, when in fact the end was not near, flies in the face of Luke 21:8. Jesus *clearly* did not want believers to say the end was near *until it was near.* This means that when He inspired them to say it was near, then, *it was truly near.*

This evidence proves that efforts to mitigate the many New Testament time statements, are wrong. God is faithful. God can tell time, and He speaks truthfully *about* time. Further, he inspired the apostles to speak truthfully about time. When they declared that the last days were present, and that the end was near, 2000 years ago, we should honor their word and reject all of the modern day prophecy "experts" whose predictions continue to fail so miserably and bring shame on the name of Christ.

The millennial school must come to grips with this indisputable fact. The dispensational school has been greatly responsible for creating a false expectation of the imminent end far too long. Lindsay said 1988 was it. He was wrong. Van Impe said 1999 was to be the year. He was wrong. LaHaye said it would be the generation that saw WW I. He was wrong. Hagee has said that this is, *without doubt* the generation that will see the end. In fact, as we have seen, he actually said that the rapture would probably occur in March of 2003. He was wrong.

Year after year we hear the same mantra, "This is the generation that will see the end of the age!"; "No generation has ever seen all of the signs of the end like this generation!" And on and on it goes.[64] We recommend that you read Francis Gummerlock's, *The Day and the Hour*, book. He chronicles the history of failed prophecies throughout the centuries.[65] Yet, year after year, prophet after prophet the predictions keep coming, and year after year, and prophet after prophet, the predictions fail. And the result is that believers become discouraged, and many become disillusioned. The skeptics and doubters scoff, and rightly so. And worse, honest hearts that want the truth witness this ongoing parade of shameful prognostications, and don't know what to believe. Some choose, as a direct result of these failed prophets who keep on proclaiming their nonsensical "escho-Babble," not to believe at all.

It is time for someone to speak up and to speak out against all of the nonsense. The men mentioned above should be held accountable for their continuing shameful failure. They need to have the integrity to stand before the Christian community, and say that they have been wrong. However, they refuse to do so, and indeed, are so bold as to blatantly misrepresent what they did say!

When the Berlin Wall fell, and Russia disintegrated, Lindsay had the unmitigated gall to appear on TBN and claim that he had predicted these events. *This is not true!* But has the dispensational community called his hand? No. He continues to write and sell books at an amazing rate. The tragedy of this can hardly be overstated.

SO, WHAT'S THE BIG DEAL ANYWAY?

You will have noticed that we have called attention to the millennial view of the last days several times. We have called the names of men like LaHaye, Ice, Jeffrey, Van Impe, Lindsay, Hagee, etc.. Why have we done this? Because there is something that you need to know, and that is that all of the sensational predictions made by these men, saying that we are in the last days, are based on one of the greatest theological errors of all time.

Did you know that all of the predictions that the end is near are based on the belief *that Jesus failed in his first mission?* That belief is that Jesus came to establish the kingdom, that Israel's last days were present in the first century, but that, due to the Jewish rejection of Jesus, the countdown of their last days was suspended. The countdown will not begin again until the so-called Rapture. At that time God will restart the prophetic clock, and will then do the second time what He could not do the first time.

Lest you think I am making this up, see the quote from Thomas Ice just below, and now read what he has to say in a new book, *The End Times*

Controversy, written to refute the ideas found in this book:[66] "The Lord made no error and clearly had 'the coming' for judgment in mind (in Matthew 10:22-23, DKP). However, the coming is contingent upon Israel's acceptance of its King. Because even after His resurrection, that nation refused Him, it became impossible to establish the kingdom (cf. Acts 3:18-26)." Did you catch that? Ice says that the Jewish rejection of Jesus made it "impossible" for God to keep His promise to establish the kingdom![67]

The contradictions in the millennial world become apparent right here. You see, on the one hand, they tell us that the Bible prophecies of the second coming were *unconditional* (*Charting*, 24), and then they tell us that the second coming was a *conditional* promise (*Controversy*, 85). Well, was it conditional or unconditional?

Further, if the promise of the second coming was conditional when the Old Testament prophets spoke it, it was conditional when the New Testament prophets spoke it. Or, did God take a conditional promise and turn it into an unconditional promise, when the conditional promise failed? If Jewish unbelief prevented the second coming in the first century, then Jewish unbelief could prevent it the second time. It also means that if the Old Testament promise of the second coming was unconditional, then it was going to happen in the first century *no matter what*; there could be no postponement.

There is another important issue here. Ice and LaHaye tell us: "prophecy is history written in advance" (*Charting*, 11), and that, "God's plan for the future is definite, well planned, and exciting. We do not live in a world of chance. Prophecy means that certain things will definitely happen, while other possibilities are eliminated." (*Prophecy*, 75). Mark

---

If God controls *what* will happen, and *when* it will happen, as the millennialists insist, then why did Jesus not complete what was predicted, when it was predicted to happen?

Hitchcock says "One of the great comforts of studying Bible prophecy is that we see the mighty, sovereign hand of God in control of all things. He controls what happens, how it happens, when it happens, and where it happens."[68]

Compare these statements that say God predetermines things to happen, controls *what will happen* and *when it will happen*, while "eliminating other possibilities," with the claim that the Jewish rejection of Jesus made it *impossible* for Jesus to accomplish what he came to do! Now, if prophecy is history written in advance, and Jesus came to establish the kingdom, how in the world did he fail to accomplish what was predicted? If God is in control of *what* happens, and *when* it happens, then why could Jesus not do what he came to do, when he came to do it? You just can't say that God controls what will happen and when it will happen, and then say that Jesus could not do *what* was predicted, *when* it was predicted to happen! If Jesus could not do what was prophesied, when it was predicted he would do it, then assuredly God did not control what would happen and when it would happen. It is just that simple.

Let's be candid about what this means. A postponed kingdom means, without doubt, *that God failed, Jesus failed, and the Bible is not the word of God!* What we are saying is that the doctrine that we are in the last days of the Christian Age, eagerly awaiting the Rapture, so that the last days of Israel can resume, is a doctrine based on the idea that God failed!

This is a strong claim, so let's take a closer look.

First, let's establish that Jesus did come at what the Bible says was "just the right time" to accomplish his mission.

The Bible says God would establish His kingdom in the days of *the Roman Empire* (Daniel 2). See the discussion above. He did not say He would establish the kingdom in a "Revived Roman Empire." That doctrine is a theological fabrication invented to explain the doctrine of Jesus' failure to do what he came to do!

Not only did the Bible set the time for the establishment of the kingdom, the Bible says that Jesus came "at just the right time" to accomplish his mission. Paul said in Galatians 4:4, that Jesus came "in the fulness of time." (See also Romans 5:6; 1 Timothy 2:6). The meaning of this is that Jesus came *at just the right time.* However, it could not have been *just the right time* if he failed!

Are we supposed to believe that the Omniscient God of the universe looked down the stream of time, and in His wisdom *thought* that He knew just the right time to send His Son, only to discover that He had *miscalculated*? Is that what we are supposed to believe about the God that knows time, space, eternity, the very thoughts of man, and all things? (See Psalms 139). What kind of a God is this, that *thought* He had chosen the right time, only to discover, "sadly," that the time was horribly wrong after all? Not only did He miscalculate the time, but His miscalculation cost Him the life of His Son, and His Son could not do what He sent him to do. Personally, I like John Anderson's view of this: "My God does not have 'oops!' in His vocabulary!"

Millennialists feel the pressure of this situation. After all, it does not speak well of a doctrine to say that God failed. So, Ice seeks to solve this by saying that Jesus' ministry actually, "Has two phases that revolve around his two comings. Phase one took place at Christ's first coming when he came in humiliation to suffer. Phase two will begin at Christ's second coming when he will reign on earth in power and glory." (*Prophecy*, 99) This simply will not work.

Notice that Ice, and this is true of most millennialists, draws a distinction between the purpose of Jesus' death, and the kingdom. In other words, according to the millennialists, Jesus did not die to establish the kingdom. He died to provide forgiveness and redemption, but one day, he will establish the kingdom. That is a totally false distinction, and yet, it is vitally important to the millennial view of things. The Biblical truth is that *Jesus died to establish the kingdom wherein is found redemption and forgiveness (Colossians 1:7-13).*

The millennialist is talking out of both sides of the mouth. On the one hand, Ice says that Jesus came to establish the kingdom, and would have done so, had the Jews accepted him. Then he turns around and tells us that Jesus did not *really* come to establish the kingdom after all. *He came to suffer.* Do you see what this means? It means that if the Jews would have accepted Jesus as their Messiah, then *Jesus would not have had to die!* The Cross stood in the way of the kingdom!

Further, if the Jews would have accepted Jesus, the kingdom would have been established, and the Cross, the foundation of redemption and salvation *would never have happened!* If the kingdom would have been established, there would be no church, no

> *According to the millennial view of things, the Cross stood in the way of the kingdom, and conversely, the kingdom would have prevented the Cross!*

forgiveness, no gospel of Grace, no glory to God in the church throughout all ages. Without the Cross, what would there be? Jew and Gentile division would remain. Without the Cross, there would be no salvation. Without the Cross, there would be *nothing*, and yet, according to the millennial view of things, it is *sad* that the Jews rejected Jesus and put him on the Cross!

This view is admitted by some millennialists. In 1983, I had a four night public debate with a premillennialist. I asked him: "If the Jews would not have crucified Jesus, would he have established the kingdom and ruled on earth?" My opponent said, "Yes, if the Jews would not have rejected him, Jesus would have established the kingdom and ruled on earth." I want the reader to ponder that thought well, for it is precisely the position that Ice and others are teaching. *The Cross stood in the way of the kingdom, and conversely, the kingdom would have prevented the Cross.* This view was openly stated by none other than one of the leading lights in the millennial movement, J. N. Darby.

Darby said that many people supposed that the Cross was the victory of God. However, he said, "It was exactly the contrary. The cross was one grand demonstration...that Satan is prince and god of this world."[69] Of course, Darby is diametrically opposed to the Bible affirmation that Jesus, "triumphed over principalities, powers and dominions" through the Cross (Colossians 2:15f; 1 Peter 3:22, etc.).

So, did Jesus come to suffer and die, *or* did he come to establish the kingdom? The millennialists see it as an either-or situation, when in reality, the Bible says he came to die, *in order to establish the kingdom.* Jesus himself directly linked his suffering with the kingdom: "Ought not the Christ to have suffered these things, and to enter into His glory?" (Luke 24:26). The context here is critical.

Jesus had been crucified, but was now resurrected. As two of his disciples walked along the road to Emmaeus, they were discouraged, and despondent. Jesus, unrecognized, joined them and asked what they were talking about. Their response is enlightening:

> "Are you the only stranger in Jerusalem, and have not known the things that have happened therein these days? And he said, 'What things?' and they said to him, 'The things concerning Jesus of Nazareth, who was a prophet mighty in deed and word before God and all the people, and how the chief priests and our rulers delivered him to be condemned to death, and crucified him. But we were hoping that it was he who was going to redeem Israel.'"

Clearly, the disciples thought Jesus was to establish the kingdom: "We thought it was he who would redeem Israel." However, *like modern millennialists,* they *thought the crucifixion had dashed their plans!* Remember, the millennialists claim that if the Jews would not have crucified Jesus, that he would have established the kingdom. This is *precisely* what the two disciples thought! This is why Jesus' response is so important: "O foolish ones, and slow of heart to believe in all that the prophets have spoken! "Ought not the Christ to have suffered these things, and to enter in His glory?"

Let me say this again. Just like the modern dispensationalists, the disciples thought the rejection of Jesus had dashed their kingdom hopes. They, like the modern millennialists, had a literalistic view of the kingdom.

They thought the cross postponed the kingdom. But Jesus' reaction was to call them *foolish* and *blind* to the scriptures. Jesus said they had failed to grasp the relationship between his suffering and the kingdom, i.e. his glory. *Jesus told them they were foolish to see the Cross as the postponement of the kingdom.* The modern student is going to have to determine who is right, Jesus, or those who view the Cross as the postponement of the kingdom

Let's establish something: *The glory of Christ is the kingdom of Christ.* This being true, this means that what Jesus was saying was that his suffering was part of the plan for him to enter into his kingdom. *The Passion was the Plan, not a postponement of the plan!*

In Matthew 20:20f, the mother of James and John came to Jesus asking, "Grant that these two sons of mine may sit, the one on Your right hand, and the other on your left, in your kingdom." Now notice the parallel passage in Mark 10:35. Mark says that the sons asked, "Grant us that we may sit, one on your right hand, and the other on your left, in Your glory." So, Jesus' kingdom is his glory, and his glory is his kingdom. Thus, when Jesus said it was necessary, and according to the prophetic scriptures, for him to suffer in order to "enter his glory," Jesus was saying that the Cross was the pathway to the Throne, not a postponement. The importance of this cannot be overemphasized. The prophecy pundits like Lindsay, Hagee, LaHaye, Van Impe, et. al., insist that *the Cross postponed the Kingdom.* Jesus said the Cross was the way for him to enter his kingdom glory! Obviously, the prophecy pundits' view of the Cross is wrong.

Jesus suffered *to enter his glory*. His glory is the *kingdom*. Thus, Jesus' suffering did not postpone the kingdom, it was the necessary prerequisite for the coming of the kingdom!

Let me repeat something important about the millennial futurist view of the Cross and kingdom. They tell us that if the Jews would have accepted Jesus, he would have established the kingdom. *This means that the acceptance of Jesus as king would have prevented the Cross.* Yet the Cross is the foundation stone of Christianity! Thus, had the kingdom been established, *Jesus would not have died.* But if Jesus had not died, there would be no salvation by grace, for that is a distinctive feature of the church. No Cross, no salvation. No Cross, no Christianity. Had the kingdom been established, the *church would never have been established.*

So, the millennialists tell us that the Cross stood in the way of the kingdom. It was God's *intent and will* to establish the kingdom. He sent Jesus to establish it. He *thought and said it was just the right time*. But, the Jews rejected Jesus, and so God had to go to "Plan B," the church, and withdrew the kingdom offer until He could figure out the *real right time*, for Jesus to come and do the second time, what he could not do the first.

What kind of a God are we talking about here? He could not see what was going to happen, so He is not Omniscient. He could not prevent what happened, nor turn it to His purpose, so He is not Omnipotent. He could not do *what* He predicted, so He *failed*. He could not keep His word at the time He predicted, so He *failed*. If the millennial view of things is correct, he is not–he can't be--God. Thankfully, the millennial view of things is wrong, and He really is GOD, for He *knew* what was going to happen, and He turned it to His purpose. He *kept His word* about *what* He was going to do, *when* He said He would do it. He did not fail. *Praise Him!*

Jesus came to establish the kingdom, and he came at *just the right time* to do so. His rejection by the Jews was not a lamentable postponement of God's kingdom plans, but God's ordained method of establishing the kingdom. Any view of the kingdom that fails or refuses to see the Cross as the road to kingdom glory is not a Biblical doctrine, and disparages the Cross of Jesus Christ. For the millennialists to say that the Church was a mystery to the prophets, unforeseen and unplanned by God until Jesus' rejection by the Jews, is simply wrong. As we have seen, the Church was the goal of all the previous ages, not a stop-gap measure on the way to the "good stuff." Jesus came at just the right time, and in the Cross, he *won*! He was not postponed. He was not frustrated. He *triumphed*, for the Cross was the pathway to the Throne.

Second, Jesus did come to establish the kingdom, and the millennialists admit this. Take a look again at what Ice says:

"I believe the scriptures teach that Israel could have obtained her much sought after messianic kingdom by recognizing Jesus as the Messiah. We all know the sad reality–the Jews rejected Jesus. As a result the kingdom is no longer near but postponed, awaiting Jewish belief, which will occur at the end of the Tribulation." (*Tribulation*, 115)

We could multiply quotes like this from all of the leading millennialists. In this statement, Ice is positively affirming that Jesus came to establish the kingdom, *but that he could not do so*. However, as a result of the Jewish rejection, "The kingdom is no longer near, but postponed." Think carefully about what is being said here!

The kingdom was near, because Jesus said it was (Mark 1:15f). By the way, by admitting that the kingdom truly was near, the millennialists are admitting that the statement "the kingdom of heaven is at hand" means exactly what it indicates. In other words, they are saying that "at hand" truly meant "at hand." This means then, that when Peter said, "The end of all things has drawn near," that the end of the age truly was at hand! If "the kingdom is at hand" meant it was near, then "the end of all things has drawn near" has to be given the same objective meaning. If not, why not?

If the Jews would have accepted it, the kingdom would have been established, per the millennial view. It was God's will, and it was Jesus' will (see Matthew 23:37), that the kingdom be established, but according to Ice, *God could not do what He sent His Son to do, and His Son could not do what he came to do!* Now, if God could not do *what* He sent Jesus to do, *when* He sent him to do it, and if Jesus could not do what he came to do, *when* he came to do it, isn't that *failure*? *What else can you call it?*

Incredibly, our dispensational friends say that the Old Testament actually predicted Jesus' failure to establish the kingdom. Daniel 9:26 predicted the death of Jesus and said, according to Ice, "Messiah shall be cut off, and have nothing." Ice asks: What was it that He (Jesus, DKP), came for but did not receive, especially in relationship to Israel and Jerusalem, which is the larger context of this overall passage? It was His Messianic kingdom! Indeed it will come, but not at the time He was cut off.' (*End Times*, 335) So, what we have is that *the millennialists claim that Daniel actually predicted the failure of Jesus' mission*!

Ice tries to make the passage say two totally different things. He says, "Certainly Christ gained what was intended through His atoning death on the cross, as far as paying for the sins of the world." (*End Times,* 335). So, Jesus accomplished *something* for the *world* in his death, but accomplished *nothing* for *Israel*. This will not do however, because if we accept the rendering "he shall have nothing," this cannot be taken to mean "he shall have *something*." Ice must accept his rendering of "nothing," or else his view has nothing! But you see, if Jesus had *nothing*, then, well, he had *nothing*! You cannot say he had *nothing*, and then insist he had *something*. But that is precisely what Ice is attempting.

Even Ice's view that Daniel 9 said Jesus accomplished something for the *world* but not for *Israel* is troublesome for the millennial view. You see, they claim that the Old Testament nowhere predicted the church or the blessings in the church. Further, they claim that Daniel 9:24-27 deals exclusively with God's promises to Israel. Well, if Daniel 9 is exclusively about Israel, then how in the world can Ice claim that Daniel 9 predicted the blessings of the atonement for the *world*, found in Christ and his *church*? How did the church wind up with the blessings of Daniel 9, (Israel's blessings!!), when Daniel 9 did not anticipate the church?

If Daniel 9 predicted the blessings of the atonement found in the church, then most assuredly, Daniel predicted the church. And that is not all. Biblically, the world would only be blessed when Israel received the fulfillment of her blessings (See Isaiah 49; 60; etc.). Scripturally, the blessing of salvation would flow from Israel to the world "to the Jew first, then to the Greek" is the divine order. Thus, to say that the world received the atonement blessing, but that Israel did not, is Biblically impossible.

The problem is that the Bible affirms in no uncertain terms that Jesus was not going to fail in his mission of establishing the kingdom. In Isaiah 42:4f, Jehovah predicted the coming of Jesus to establish the kingdom, and promised this, "He shall not fail nor be discouraged til He has established justice in the earth." So, the millennialist says that Daniel predicted the failure of Jesus, but Isaiah said that Jesus would not fail in his mission. Who will you believe?

President Bush sent American troops into Iraq with the stated goal of removing the regime of Saddam Hussein. He said it was going to be done shortly, "the end of the tyrant's rule is at hand" was his promise. Well, had the Iraqis repelled the American invasion, and Saddam Hussein remained in power, could Bush say, "We have succeeded in our mission"? Everyone would know that he was acting as the Iraqi information, minister, Baghdad Bob as he was known, who, with American planes in the air over head as he spoke, claimed that the Americans were in full retreat, and "committing suicide by the hundreds!" It is called *spin*, (it is also called being in *denial*!), and is nothing but a denial of reality! Thus, if Jesus came to do something, and it was just the right time to do it, then if he did not do it, *he failed*. You can't *spin* it any other way.

If God could not do *what* He said He would do, *when* He said He would do it, *then God failed*! This is undeniable.

We have to take note right here of a *major contradiction* in the millennial view. As we just saw, the millennialists claim that Jesus did come to establish the kingdom. But, did you know that they also say he did not come to establish the kingdom? Read carefully the following comments:–"The purpose of his first coming was to announce the period of grace and salvation we are living in, not the time of judgment that is yet to come." (*Charting*, 30). In that same work, Ice and LaHaye claim:

> "The major reason many people rejected Jesus was ... because he had not thrown off the shackles of Roman dictators. They wanted him to free Israel, yet did not realize the prophecies related to his future kingdom would be fulfilled at his second coming, and not his first. He came instead to suffer for their sins, die on the cross, and rise again–without which there would be no forgiveness of sins, or eternal life." (*Charting*, 26)

So there you have it. On the one hand Jesus came to establish the kingdom, and if the Jews had recognized him, he would have done so. On the other hand, he did *not* come to establish the kingdom in the first place! Well, if Jesus did not even come to establish the kingdom at his first coming, then why do the dispensational authors speak of the "sad reality" of the rejection and crucifixion of Christ that "postponed" the kingdom offer? If Jesus did not come to establish the kingdom, then he most assuredly did not have to withdraw the kingdom offer and postpone it until the Second Coming. This is a major contradiction!

So, what we have in points #1 and 2 is this: The Bible set the time for the establishment of the kingdom, i.e. the days of the Roman Empire. Jesus came in the days of the Roman Empire, to establish the kingdom. Jesus not only came during the time foretold for the establishment of the kingdom, he said the predicted time was fulfilled (Mark 1:15). And, not only did Jesus say that the time was fulfilled, the Bible says he came "*at just the right time,*" he came, "in the fulness of the time" (Romans 5:6f; Galatians 4:4, etc). So, according to the Bible, Jesus came at what God thought was just the right time to establish the kingdom.

Unfortunately, says the millennialists, Jesus could not establish the kingdom because the Jews rejected him. We could say a lot about this, but suffice it to say that *the Jews did not reject Jesus as king, until Jesus had rejected the Jews' offer for him to be king.*

The Jews did not reject Jesus as king, until Jesus had rejected the Jews' offer for him to be king! **Why?**

In John 6:15, Jesus had fed the multitude, and the crowd was wildly enthusiastic thinking they saw in Jesus the one to lead them to national restoration. However, read Jesus' response: "When Jesus perceived that they were about to come and take him by force to make him king, he departed again to a mountain by Himself alone." This is one of the most ignored verses in the Bible in the discussion of the establishment of the kingdom and the last days. Why? Because it proves that the Jews did not reject Jesus until Jesus had rejected their offer of the kingdom.

The question is *Why?* Why did Jesus reject this offer of kingship? Did he not come to be king? Yes! Why then reject the offer to be king? Did he not come to establish the kingdom? Yes! Why then reject the offer of the kingdom? If the Jews were offering what Jesus wanted, why did Jesus reject it? And, if Jesus was actually offering what the Jews wanted why would they later reject him?

We must interject an important fact. We often say that Israel rejected Jesus, when in fact, *true Israel* accepted him. Historically, there has always been an "Israel within Israel" reality. We sometimes call this "inner Israel" the *remnant*. These are the faithful ones of Israel that, even in the worst of times, maintained their faith in Jehovah, and walked humbly before Him. In the New Testament, Jesus identified those who followed him as the true people of God (John 15:1f). Paul said the remnant, i.e. the elect, were obtaining the promises of God, but of course, the remnant he alludes to were the Jews who were accepting Jesus as Messiah (Romans 9-11). Peter went so far as to say that those who rejected Jesus would be "cut off from the people" (Acts 3:24). That is, those who rejected Jesus as Messiah would no longer be considered "the people." We cannot develop this further, but this is a vital issue being virtually ignored. The millennial view seems to have no grasp of this topic.

The only answer to these questions is that *Jesus did not want the kind of kingdom and kingship they were offering.* Had they both been offering what the other wanted, there is no logical, sensible explanation for Jesus to reject them, and them to later reject him.

Here is something that is normally ignored by our millennial friends in their zeal for a restored nationalistic kingdom. It is the fact that a physical king sitting on a literal throne was, from its inception, *a symbol of Israel's rejection of God!* Did you catch that? Let me repeat that, it is really important. The desire for a physical king sitting on a literal throne in Jerusalem, ruling over the nation of Israel, was, from its inception, a symbol of Israel's rejection of Jehovah.

In 1 Samuel 8, as Israel was living in the land during the period of the judges, the people grew jealous of the nations surrounding them, with their pomp and ceremony surrounding the kingly courts. So, they approached Samuel, God's prophet and judge, and requested that he anoint a king over Israel. Samuel was devastated. He took this request as a personal insult and rejection. However, God saw it in a different light. Jehovah said to Samuel:

> "Heed the voice of the people in all that they say to you: for they have not rejected you, but they have rejected Me, that I should not reign over them. According to all the works which they have done since the day that I brought them up out of the land of Egypt, even to this day–with which they have forsaken Me and served other gods–so they are doing to you also." (1 Samuel 8:7-8).

Please note a couple of powerful points:

A.) God said that Israel's desire for a physical king was a *rejection of Him*. Now, unless you can show that in some other passage before this, God ever expressed a desire to establish a physical king on a literal throne, then we have to take His word for it, that Israel's desire for a physical king was an open rejection of God!

The desire for a physical king on a literal throne was, from the beginning, a sign of Israel's rebellion and rejection of God. Did Jesus come to re-establish that symbol of rebellion?

B.) God said that this desire for a physical king was a continuance of Israel's pattern of rebellion, and disobedience that went all the way back to the Exodus. Jehovah placed Israel's desire for a nationalistic king on the same level as idolatry! He said it was a continuance of their habit of "forsaking" Him. Be sure to read 1 Samuel 10:19 and 12:17f where Samuel called Israel's desire for a physical king a "great sin" and "evil" as well.

Now, if Jehovah said the desire for a physical king was a sign of Israel's rejection of His sovereignty, is it any wonder that Jesus rejected the offer of a literal, nationalistic kingship?[70] Would not the restoration of a physical king be the restoration of that symbol of rebellion? *Did Jesus come to re-establish the symbol of rebellion against Jehovah's sovereignty?* The fact is, it was *never* God's intent for the Messiah to sit on a physical throne, on earth, ruling over a political and national kingdom.

Furthermore, John Anderson astutely notes that in Jesus' temptation, Jesus had the first of two offers of a national kingdom. Did not Satan offer Jesus, "all the kingdoms of this world and their glory" (Matthew 4:8)?

Were those not national, political kingdoms? He surely was not offering Jesus the church! Now, in Matthew, Satan offered Jesus all of the kingdoms, and in John the Jews offered him their kingdom, *but Jesus rejected all offers of physical kingship!* If Jesus would have accepted the offer in Matthew, he would have been in rebellion against his Father. And, the nationalistic king over Israel was a symbol of rejection of God. Thus, had Jesus accepted either offer to be a physical king, *he would have been in rebellion against the Father!* Does that not tell us something about the kind of kingdom Jesus really wanted?

This has powerful implications. When did the concept of a political king ever become idealistic in the mind of Jehovah? In the book of Hosea, Jehovah pleaded with Israel to return to the former days before a political king sat on the throne. He said:

> "O Israel, you are destroyed but your help is from me. I will be your king; where is any other that he may save you...I gave you a king in My anger and took him away in my wrath" (Hosea 13:9-10).

You see, *a nationalistic king was not God's original–or continuing-- intent for His people.* This is why Jesus rejected that offer in the Great Temptation and in John 6. Does not his rejection of those offers make it clear he did not come to restore that symbol of rebellion? We suggest that Jesus was very aware of 1 Samuel 8:7f.

Further, while Jesus rejected their offer of a kingship, he did offer to be their king. However they rejected his offer. Isn't it pretty clear that Jesus was not offering them what they wanted?

So, in our first two points, we have shown that Jesus came *at just the right time*, and that he came *to establish the kingdom*. Don't we have a right to ask, If he came at the right time, and he came do establish the kingdom, then why didn't he do what he came to do? Now to the third point to help answer that question.

Third, the Bible says *God would not change His kingdom plans*, and Jesus would not fail in the kingdom plans. Thus, for anyone to teach that God did change his plans, or that Jesus did not accomplish his mission, *is an outright denial of God's word.* Take note of three important passages.
1.) Psalms 2:4 – "Why do the nations rage, and the people plot a vain thing? The kings of the earth set themselves, and the rulers take counsel together, against the Lord and against His anointed, saying, 'Let us break their bonds in pieces, and cast away their cords from us.'" This text spoke of God's determination to enthrone His Son on the Holy Hill Zion. This is just another way of saying that He was going to establish the kingdom.

However, man would attempt to thwart His purpose. What would be God's response to man's efforts? God would *laugh* at the efforts of man to thwart His plan to enthrone the king. If God had to postpone the kingdom, due to the tragic crucifixion of His Son, would He have laughed at that?

Notice that verse 6 said, "Yet have I set my King on my Holy Hill Zion." Do you get the force of that? Man would try to prevent it by rejecting the Son, but God *laughed* at man's attempt to thwart the kingdom plan by crucifying Jesus. Notice the word, "Yet!" *What a word! Their* efforts were futile, not *His*!

Look at Luke 10. Jesus sent his disciples to preach,"The kingdom of God has drawn near" (v. 10). He *knew* that Israel was not going to be receptive, and warned his disciples of this. But in one of the most ignored verses in the Bible Jesus said, "But whatever city you enter, and they do not receive you, go out into its streets and say, 'The very dust of your city which clings to us we wipe off against you. Nevertheless know this, that the kingdom of God has come near you!'" (v. 10-11). Did you catch that? *Jesus told his disciples that their offer of the kingdom to Israel was going to be rejected.* Did he tell them to tell their audiences, "Take heed lest the kingdom offer be postponed"? No. Did he instruct his disciples to say, "If you don't accept the kingdom offer now, the offer will be withdrawn for over 2000 years until another faithful generation arises"? No. Did Jesus indicate in any way that the kingdom offer was going to be altered, postponed, or withdrawn? No, and this is important, because as John Anderson likes to point out, Amos 3:7 says: "Surely the Lord does nothing, unless He reveals His secret to His servants the prophets."

If Jesus was going to postpone the kingdom due to the rebellion of the Jews, then he should have, according to Amos, instructed the disciples to warn Israel that her rejection was going to lead to the postponement of her kingdom hopes. Yet, there is not one verse in the Bible that says the kingdom was postponed. There is not one Old Testament verse that indicates that the kingdom would be delayed. Instead, as Psalms 2 and the verses we are about to examine show, God knew that Israel was going to reject His offer, but God would not be deterred. God would not be defeated. God would not fail, and He would not alter His plans. So, since Amos says that God would not do anything without revealing it to His prophets, and since He never said one word about a delayed kingdom, that means the kingdom was not going to be, and was not, postponed.

Instead of telling his disciples to warn Israel that her kingdom could be postponed by their disobedience, Jesus told his disciples to tell their unreceptive audiences: "Nevertheless, know this, that the kingdom of God has drawn near!" Notice the power of *nevertheless*. It says that in spite of their rejection, in spite of their disobedience, in spite of their rebellion, God was going to establish the kingdom anyway! *"Nevertheless,"* just like *"yet,"* has tremendous power!

> **"Nevertheless the kingdom has drawn near to you" means that the kingdom was near *in spite of their rejection!* They could not postpone the kingdom!**

Note that Jesus said, *"Nevertheless*, the kingdom of God *has come near you."* *Nevertheless* means, "You can't keep it from coming, it has drawn near!" *Nevertheless* says God's purpose will not be postponed. *Nevertheless* says it is near in spite of your rejection. This is exactly the *opposite* of what the millennial view needed for him to say. They *needed* for Jesus to tell his disciples to inform the rebels that their recalcitrance was going to postpone the kingdom. The millennial view *needed* for Jesus to tell his disciples to warn Israel that if they did not recognize Jesus as their king, that the kingdom would "no longer be near." The millennial doctrine *needed* for Jesus to have his disciples tell Israel that if their generation missed their chance, that the kingdom offer would be withdrawn for thousands of years before God offered the kingdom again.

We have to say something more here about this postponed kingdom idea. Everyone admits that the Bible says certain things had to occur before the establishment of the kingdom. Certain signs had to occur. See our discussion of the signs below. For brevity, the millennial view of things is that God's schema for the establishment of the kingdom is as follows:

1.) The end of the current Christian Age at the Rapture.

2.) The signing of the peace treaty between Israel and the Anti-christ.

3.) The rebuilding of a temple in Jerusalem.

4.) The revival of Judaism, and the restoration of animal sacrifices and ceremonies.

5.) The Russian army invades Israel, but is mysteriously destroyed.

6.) The newly proclaimed world emperor (The Man of Sin), desecrates the Temple in Jerusalem, and begins to persecute the Jews. (The Great Tribulation)

7.) Many Jews recognize the unfolding of prophetic events and declare their faith in Jesus as Messiah.

8.) In the massacre of Jews and Christians who resist the world dictator, some witnesses are divinely preserved to carry the message to the world. (Elijah is supposed to come then as well, DKP)

9.) Christ returns to earth, (Second Coming), welcomed by believing Jews as their Messiah and deliverer.

10.) Christ's thousand-year reign on earth from the throne of David finally fulfills the prophetic promises to the nation of Israel. (*Prophecy*, 60) This is the establishment of the kingdom *at the end of Daniel's 70 Weeks.*

Okay, with this in mind, let's take a closer look at the idea that the kingdom was postponed. We have already taken note that the millennial school admits that Jesus and John said *the kingdom had drawn near.* See Ice's quote again. There can be no doubt about this. Now, what this means is, if the kingdom was near, *then the end of the Christian Age was near,* Elijah was near, the completion of the World Mission was near, the Tribulation was near, the Man of Sin was near, etc.. If the kingdom was truly near, *as all millennialists admit, then this means that all of these events were to occur in that generation!*

There are lots of problems with this. Can you imagine Jesus saying that the end of the Christian Age, which is absolutely necessary for the kingdom to be near, had drawn near? How in the world could the end of the Christian Age be near, when the Church Age had not even begun yet? Let's take a look at this logically.

The end of the Christian Age is necessary for the establishment of the kingdom to draw near (millennial view).

But the kingdom had drawn near when Jesus was alive (Matthew 3:2; Mark 1:15-17).

Conclusion: Therefore, the end of the Christian Age had drawn near when Jesus was alive.

You can't just say the kingdom had drawn near without at the same time saying that all of the necessary prerequisites for the establishment of the kingdom were near as well. The establishment of the kingdom was not to occur in a vacuum. Don't our millennial friends constantly tell us the end of the present age is at hand, and therefore the kingdom is at hand? Well, if the Christian Age has to end before the kingdom can be established, then undeniably, when Jesus said: "The kingdom of heaven has drawn near," he must have been saying the end of the Christian Age was near as well!

It is obvious that the end of the Christian Age was not near when Jesus spoke -*it had not even begun!*-and the end of the Christian Age was not near at *any time* in the first century. Nor will the end of the Christian Age *ever* be near, *because the Christian Age has no end!* That means that the only "end" that could have been near was the end of the Jewish Age.

Biblically, the coming of the kingdom is at the *end of the Jewish Age (Hebrews 9:6-10)*. For Jesus to say the kingdom was near meant the end of Jewish Age was near. The millennialists say that Israel's last days are in the future. However, the Old World of Israel *did end* with the fall of Jerusalem in A.D. 70. This is powerful evidence that the end of the Jewish Age, *the end of the 70 Weeks*, really was near, and not postponed.

Consider this: for the millennialists to admit that Jesus said the kingdom truly was near, means that we can take the time statements of the Bible at face value. At hand really did mean *at hand.* However, if we take the time statements about the nearness of the kingdom seriously, then we must also take the time statements in the rest of the Bible seriously when they say that the end of the age was near.

Jesus said that John the Baptizer was Elijah (Matthew 11; Matthew 17). But, if the kingdom was postponed, then for John to be Elijah, he–not literal Elijah--has to be resurrected at some point in the future to play the role of Elijah again. So you see, the idea of a postponed kingdom has severe consequences, that are simply ludicrous to suggest.

Did Jesus say that the *end* of the Church Age had drawn near, before the Christian Age had even *begun*?

If the kingdom was near, but postponed, then the completion of the World Mission was truly supposed to be a first century event. Why didn't the inspired writers say that the fulfillment of the Mission was now delayed? Why did they say the Mission *had been fulfilled*, in their generation, and that the end was near? (See Romans 16:20, 25-26, Colossians 1:5-7, 23, etc.) The inspired writers knew *nothing* of a postponed fulfillment of the Great Commission.

If the kingdom was near, but postponed, then the Great Tribulation really was supposed to be a first century generation event, but was postponed. Now, if Jesus said the kingdom had drawn near, why don't we just accept his word in Matthew 24:15-34 when he spoke of the Great Tribulation, and said it was to occur in his generation. The fact that he said the kingdom was near proves that the Great Tribulation was supposed to be in that generation. Why deny his words in Matthew when he emphatically said it belonged to that generation (Matthew 24:34).

If the kingdom was near, but postponed, this means that the Man of Sin was alive in the first century, *but his appearance was postponed*, for what has now been 2000 years! In fact, Paul said the Man of Sin was alive and well in the first century (2 Thessalonians 2:5f). Now, if the Man of Sin is an individual, and was near in the first century, then clearly he had to have died in the interim between the first century and now, but he will one day be raised from the dead.

As you can see, *if the kingdom was postponed*, it means that not only was the kingdom postponed, *but each of the preceding events was postponed as well!* Do you see some of the problems of saying the kingdom was postponed? As we have seen, you can't simply say that the kingdom was postponed without demanding, logically, *that all of the preceding signs of the kingdom had to be postponed as well.* But, if they were postponed, then that means *they were originally scheduled for the first century.* If they were originally appointed for the first century, but did not occur, then we are back to the failure of God, Christ and the apostles.

> You can't simply say that the kingdom was postponed without demanding, logically, *that all of the preceding signs of the kingdom were postponed as well*

Here is a highly significant point. There is not one verse in the New Testament that hints or suggests that the kingdom had been postponed. Now, think of how fundamental the doctrine of the postponed kingdom is to today's so-called prophecy experts. The doctrine is so important that Ice says if there is no postponement doctrine then there is no such thing as dispensationalism. Think about that and then think about the fact that not one, I repeat, *not one verse* in the New Testament speaks of "the delay of God's kingdom plan." Not one verse speaks of the gap between Daniel's 69th and 70th week. Don't you think, if the postponement doctrine were so Biblical and so important, that at least *one* New Testament writer would have mentioned it? Instead of saying the kingdom had been postponed however, Jesus told his disciples to tell rebellious Israel, "Nevertheless, the kingdom of heaven has drawn near!"

Luke 10 thus becomes vitally important in understanding the predictions of the kingdom, and whether or not God would postpone it. Jesus did not tell his disciples to speak of an altered promise and a delayed kingdom. He told them to say that *in spite of the Jew's rebellion* the kingdom was near. This means that their rebellion did not postpone the kingdom, or alter God's plans. It means that God laughed at their rebellion, and in fact, used their rebellion–as instruments of wrath–to accomplish His divine purpose. God laughed! God kept His Word! And as the next verse shows, He did not *change* His promise in anyway.

2.) Psalms 89:34f :

> "My covenant I will not break, nor alter the word that has gone out of My lips. Once have I sworn in my Holiness I will not lie to David. His seed shall endure forever as the sun before Me; is shall be established like the moon, Even as a faithful witness in the sky."

Jehovah said it was His purpose to set the seed of David, the Messiah, on David's throne. Further, *God said He would not alter those plans.* Is the *timing* a part of the plan and prediction? It is *fundamentally important* in the prophecies of Daniel 2, 7, and 9. If the timing is a vital part of the program, and if the timing is altered, then the kingdom plan was altered, and God broke His word!

So, if Jesus came to establish the kingdom, and honestly offered the kingdom to the Jews the first time, if he did not establish the kingdom, but will do it the second time, *then God did alter his promise!* Furthermore, consider this. If there is a gap of so far 2000 years in the text of Daniel 9, then this means that *the kingdom was not supposed to be established in the first century after all.* Of course, as we have seen, the millennialists insist that *Jesus did come to establish the kingdom at his first coming.*

However, this will not work. If there is a gap between the 69th and 70th Week then the Divine Plan was that the kingdom would not be established before the end of the 70th Weeks, which is, we are told, yet future. Okay, if it was not God's Divine Plan to establish the kingdom until the yet future end of the 70th Week, then if Jesus would have established the kingdom in the first century, as the millennialists say he would had the Jews accepted him, this means that *the establishment of the kingdom in the first century would have been an alteration of God's plan.*

So, *if there is a gap in Daniel 9, then the establishment of the kingdom in the first century would have altered God's plan.* However, *if there is no gap*, then the postponement of the kingdom altered God's plan. Either way, the millennial doctrine says that God altered His kingdom plans, and *God said He would not do that!* There is no way around this.

As mentioned earlier, in 1983 I debated a dispensational minister. He argued that just because God *postponed* the establishment of the kingdom from the first coming to the second, this did not mean that He had actually altered His word. I posed the following illustration to the audience.

Suppose that you tell your wife that the family is going to go on a fabulous vacation to Hawaii. However, due to the expense, the family is going to have to scratch and save for 10 years. The family is excited. The date is set and circled on the calendar. Time passes, and with effort, the funds begin to accumulate. Five years pass, then seven, then nine. The months slowly pass until there is only one week left until the anticipated vacation. Then, the day before the family is to leave, the Father walks into the living room and says, "Guys, I hate to tell you this, but due to unforeseen circumstances, we won't get to leave tomorrow for our vacation. It is going to be around 20 more years before we can leave. But hey, don't worry, *this is not a change of plans!*" Do you suppose *you* could convince *your* family that you had not altered the plans, *radically*?

There is no other way to look at it. If God set the time for the establishment of the kingdom, *and He did*, then if He postponed the establishment of the kingdom for what is now 2000 years, then He changed, altered and modified His original promise.

We can't move on just yet without taking note of something. Remember Ice's statement that there were to be two phases of Jesus' ministry? Here is his quote again: "Christ's ministry has two phases that revolve around his two comings. Phase one took place at Christ's first coming when he came in humiliation to suffer. Phase two will begin at Christ's second coming when he will reign on earth in power and glory." (*Prophecy*, 99) Do you see what this means? It means, without doubt, that Jesus was not supposed to actually establish the kingdom and reign on earth until the Second Coming. But, this is major trouble for the millennial view.

Did Jesus come to establish the kingdom? If he came to establish the kingdom at his first coming, then it was not *supposed* to be established at the second coming. But, if he was supposed to establish the kingdom *at the first coming*, then did the rejection of his kingdom offer create the necessity of the Second Coming? In other words, would the Second Coming have ever been a part of God's plan if Jesus would have established the kingdom when he came the first time? If the millennialist says that God's plan was always to establish the kingdom at *the Second Coming*, then Jesus did not *honestly* offer the kingdom to Israel at his first coming. You cannot logically say that Jesus was supposed to establish the kingdom at his first coming, and then turn around and say that he was *not* supposed to do it then, but at his Second Coming. So, was Jesus supposed to establish the kingdom at the first coming?

> **You cannot logically say that Jesus was supposed to establish the kingdom at his *first* coming, and then turn around and say that he was not supposed to do it then, but at his Second Coming!**

Take a look again at what Ice says: "I believe the scriptures teach that Israel could have obtained her much sought after messianic kingdom by recognizing Jesus as the Messiah. We all know the sad reality–the Jews rejected Jesus. As a result the kingdom is no longer near but postponed, awaiting Jewish belief, which will occur at the end of the Tribulation." (*Tribulation*, 115) So, Jesus *did* come to establish the kingdom, but not *really*, because he actually came to suffer, and his suffering has nothing to do with the kingdom!

You just have to catch the power of this contradiction. The kingdom really was near at Jesus' first coming. Jesus really did offer the kingdom at that time, but they rejected it. So, it was postponed until the Second Coming, because the plan from the beginning was for him to establish the kingdom at his Second Coming!

The bottom line to this is the idea that Jesus came to do something, *but he could not do it.* What was supposed to be "just the right time" turned out to be *just the wrong time.* Jesus was horribly, tragically mistaken to proclaim, "The time is fulfilled, the kingdom of heaven is at hand."

Yet, this view of things is the exact opposite of what God said. He said He was going to laugh at man's rebellion. He said He was not going to alter the conditions of His promise. God's promise to establish the kingdom, and God's *time* to establish the kingdom were *unconditional promises.* God said He was going to do something, and He said He was not going to change His promises. It is a theological tragedy to say that He failed to keep His word, and that He changed what He said He would not change.

Consider this. The millennialists insist that God will do the second time what He failed to do the first: "That which was rejected at the time of his first coming will now be accepted and fully realized as He reigns on earth for a 1000 years." (Prophecy, 260). *And just why should we believe this?* If man's unbelief thwarted God the first time, what prevents that same unbelief from preventing His success the second time? It is responded that this time, it is God's sovereignty, His *Will* and majesty, that will succeed. Well, was God not sovereign at Jesus' first coming? Was it not truly His will to establish the kingdom the first time around? If the sovereignty of

God ensures success the second time, why did it not ensure success the first? We turn now to the third of the passages we want to examine.

3.) Isaiah 42:4f – "He shall not fail nor be discouraged until He has established justice and judgment in the earth." This is undeniably a Messianic kingdom text. Please note that *it does not say*, "He will not fail *the second time he tries* to establish justice and judgment." Could God not see the postponement of the first attempt? If Jehovah could see that man was going to refuse Jesus' kingdom offer (Psalms 2), and sent him to establish the kingdom *anyway*, and said *he would not fail in his mission*, isn't it pretty clear that the Jewish rejection of Jesus did not postpone the kingdom?

The fact that Jehovah said that His Messiah *would not fail* in his mission to establish the kingdom means that the foundation of modern day millennialism is rotten to the core, because, all of the modern day prognostications of the end, are based on Jesus' failure at the beginning.

The power of Isaiah 42 can hardly be over emphasized. The fact that Jehovah said that His Messiah was going to establish the kingdom, and that *he would not fail* in his mission means that the foundation of modern day millennialism is rotten to the core, because, all of the modern day prognostications of the end, are based on Jesus' failure at the beginning.

These three Old Testament prophecies of Jesus establish some vitally important facts.

First, God knew in advance that the Jews would reject His son, and attempt to thwart His Kingdom purpose (Psalms 2). However, God would laugh at their attempts.

Second, God said that He *would not alter* the promise to sit David's descendant on the throne. We have seen that God promised *when* He would do that. Jesus came, "at just the right time," and, he came to establish the kingdom.[71] Thus, if Jesus came at just the right time, to establish the kingdom, and if God said He would not alter His plans, if Jesus did not do what he came to do, then God's promise failed! This is unavoidable!

Third, God said, not only that He would not alter His Kingdom promises, but that *Jesus would not fail.*

Now, if Jehovah knew, before He ever sent Jesus, that the Jews were going to reject Him, but, in *full knowledge* of that coming rejection, sent him to establish the kingdom anyway, does it not follow that He was going to use that rejection as part of His plan to establish the kingdom? If God knew in advance, that the Jews were going to reject Jesus' kingdom offer, but He sent him anyway, and said it was *"just the right time,"* then does it not follow that God knew precisely what He was doing, and that Jesus' rejection was in fact a part of the kingdom plan?

The only way for the modern postponement theory to be true is if God did not know that the Jews would reject His Son, so that, when they did, He had to alter His plan. But remember, the prophecies said *He did know* they were going to reject him, and He said he was not going to alter His plans. His Son would not fail!

IF YOUR THEOLOGY SAYS THAT GOD FAILED, YOU NEED TO CHANGE YOUR THEOLOGY!

So, what have we seen in this section? We have seen that the foundation of the modern day "prophecy experts" like LaHaye, Van Impe, Ice, Hagee, etc. is false. They say that Jesus came to do something, but couldn't, so it was postponed.

We have seen however, that God knew beforehand that man would reject Jesus, but sent him anyway, at what He called "just the right time." Further, God said that He was not going to alter His kingdom plans. Yet, the millennialists say He did just that! Finally, we have seen that God said Jesus would not fail in his mission, while the entire doctrine of the modern day so-called experts is built on the theory that *Jesus did fail* the first time!

Do you really want to serve a God that could not plan any better than that? Do you want a God who vacillates so radically? Do you want a God that can be so easily thwarted in His plans? Do you want to serve a God that says He is going to do one thing, but does something entirely different. Might I kindly suggest that if you believe in a God that failed, then you need to change your theology! Take to heart the words of Isaiah 42: *"He shall not fail!"*

SO WHAT DOES ALL THIS MEAN, ANYWAY?

Okay, you might be thinking, what does all of this mean? If Jesus did not fail, what does that mean for us today? And, if all of this wild forecasting of the future is just so much hot air, what does that mean for you and for me, as we face the future. Well, as a matter of fact, it means a lot! And, this is very important, it means good things!

First, if God kept His promise to establish the kingdom, then that means that we can trust His word.

Second, if Jesus kept his word to establish the kingdom, then we can trust him as the Son of God.

Third, if the kingdom was established in the first century as the New Testament writers affirm, then we can trust the Bible as reliable and authoritative.

Of course, on the negative side of this, if God did not keep His word, and if Jesus failed, and if the New Testament writers were wrong in their expectations and predictions, then, quite simply Christianity is falsified and is a horrible hoax.

Fourth, if the last days really were in the first century, and ended at the fall of Jerusalem in AD 70, as we have shown, then the entire premillennial house of cards falls to the ground. This means that the book selling kingdoms of men like Lindsay, LaHaye, Ice, and all of the other sensationalistic "prophets" are producing nothing but theological fiction.

Fifth, and this is *really good news*, if the last days were in the first century, and the last days prophecies have been fulfilled, then the kingdom of God has been established. This means that now, those who are in Christ and obey him have eternal life and fellowship with the Father. It means that man can have a relationship with God that physical death does not sever. It means that man can be forgiven and stand pure, redeemed and sanctified by the blood of Jesus Christ.

Some may say that these blessings could be had before the end of the age. This is partially true. We cannot develop these ideas here, but suffice it to say that the Bible speaks of salvation, redemption, atonement, etc. as an "already-but-not-yet." This is widely recognized among Bible students. What is overlooked is that the "not yet" is invariably said to be near by the New Testament writers, and that it was coming at the end of the age. They were anticipating the completion of the salvation process that had been *initiated* at the Cross, but was to be perfected at the end of the age.

If the end of the age has not come, if we are either in the last days, or waiting for the coming of the last days and the end of the age, then there is no way out of this fact, *salvation is not a present reality*. Eternal life is but a promise. The atoning work of Christ has not been finished, and man can but wait with fear for the consummation.

However, the realization that God has finished His work, and that, "all things that are written" were fulfilled in the passing of the Old Covenant World of Israel in AD 70 (Luke 21:22), shows that salvation is now completed, and man can, if he wills, be restored into the presence of God! And that, my friend, is *good news*!

Sixth, more good news, if the last days were in the first century, and focused on Israel's last days, and not the end of time, then this means several things.

A.) It means that the Abomination of Desolation is not for our generation. Is that good news or bad?

B.) It means that the Great Tribulation is not for our generation or for our future at all! Is that good news or bad? Would it trouble you to know that over two thirds of the earth's population *will not be destroyed* in a holocaust of unparalleled proportions brought on the by the Man of Sin?

C.) It means that the Man of Sin is not in our future. Is that bad news?

D.) It means that the Mark of the Beast is not in our future. This means that all of those well intentioned, but misguided folks that have this morbid fear of bar-codes, social security cards, ID chips, computers, and what not, can relax! The number 666 was fulfilled, and has nothing to do with your computer, or the Wal-Mart bar code scanners. Is that good news or bad?

E.) It means that America can re-examine its foreign policy toward Israel, based solely on military, political and security reasons, and not on misguided theological reasons. In April of 2002, Jim Inhofe, U. S. senator from Oklahoma, gave a speech on the senate floor, and stated that America must support Israel at all costs because she is God's chosen people and the land belongs to her. Hal Lindsay, Jerry Falwell and other so-called prophecy experts are saying that if America does not support Israel at all costs she will be destroyed.

However, the realization that Old Covenant Israel is no longer God's chosen nation, (Old Covenant Israel no longer exists.), and that, therefore, the curses pronounced against those who did not support her are now abrogated, allows us to take a close look at our policies. It might well be that America needs to support Israel based on purely political, national, security reasons, and if that is the case, then that is fine. However, it is *wrong* to blindly support her based on the fallacious view that the world is headed toward the last days in which modern Israel remains the focus of God's plan.

Seventh, in short, if the last days have been fulfilled, then the future can be bright, *if* we will seize onto the Truth! Dispensational premillennialism is one of the most negative, frightful, pessimistic views ever invented. One dispensational author was asked if Christians should engage in political actions to help change the world and make it a better place. His response was, "You don't polish brass on a sinking ship!"

Now, the millennialists don't like this charge of "pessimillennialism" claiming that their message is actually one of hope and encouragement. However, while they spend literally millions of dollars to help transport Jewish immigrants back to Israel, what they are not telling those immigrants is that in the millennial view of things, two thirds of them are doomed to perish in the Great Tribulation that is just around the corner!

The millennialists can talk about their positive theology all they want, but the prospect of half or more of the world's population being killed doesn't sound very enticing. They can talk about the promise of the kingdom all they want, but their emphasis on the Great Tribulation which will supposedly make all of the World Wars look like picnics, has a tendency to focus on doom, death and destruction.

By the way, we have to point out that the amillennial view of things, the view I personally held for a good part of my life, is also essentially negative. After all, it is said, "evil men and seducers shall wax worse and worse, deceiving and being deceived" (2 Timothy 3). The church can't really do anything about the world conditions, so just sit back and wait for the end of the age when God will take care of everything. This is not a positive theology!

Postmillennialism comes closer to having more of a positive theology of the future, but even this is tainted with the expectation that this earth will one day be destroyed and time will end.

The point is, that if the last days were truly in the first century as this book has shown, there is no need to fear the future. Are we being "Polly Annish," and refusing to acknowledge the evil and suffering that is in the world? Not at all. We are painfully and acutely aware of the horrible atrocities that abound in our world. The terrorist attacks by Moslem fanatics are very real, very painful, very threatening.

However, do you realize that a lot of the problems like this come back to theological views about Israel and the last days? Are you aware that America is hated for her support of Israel? Of course, America says she must support Israel because she is supposed to be God's chosen people. Do you see how *theology is impacting our world*? Do you see how one's view of the end of the age becomes so critical and important?

What we are suggesting is that the proper view of the last days, and therefore of Israel, can and should have a profound and *positive* impact on our view of the world, and the future. The realization that the future is not full of doom and destruction perpetrated by some mad, demonic Man of Sin should encourage everyone. In other words, the future can be bright if we will make it that way, based on proper thinking about the end of the age. Is that good news or bad?

SUMMARY AND CONCLUSION

So, what have we seen in this book?

First, we have identified the term "last days" as a referent to the last days of Israel's Old Covenant World. The term *last days* does not refer to the last days of time, or the last days of the Christian Age.

Second, we have shown that Jesus and the New Testament writers said that the end of the age was to occur in their generation. Virtually all of the New Testament writers tell us that the things foretold by the Old Testament writers, who spoke of Israel's last days, were being fulfilled in their day. We have shown that the Old Testament writers foretold the last days of Israel. Therefore, when the New Testament writers said that what the Old Covenant prophets foretold was present, we can be sure that the New Testament writers were speaking of the last days of Israel. Unless it can be shown that Old Covenant prophets foretold the end of the Christian Age, then since the New Testament writers were anticipating the end of the age foretold by the Old Covenant prophets, we must conclude that neither the Old Prophets or the New spoke of the end of the Christian Age.

Third, we have shown that the last days of Israel came to an end at the destruction of Jerusalem in A.D. 70.

Fourth, we have shown that the theology of the modern day prophecy experts like Lindsay, LaHaye, Hagee, et. al., is based on a theological horror. That is, that *Jesus failed* in his mission and the kingdom was postponed. We have shown that God said He would laugh at man's attempt to defeat His plans, that He would not alter His plan, and that Jesus would not fail. Yet, in spite of this, the popular preachers just named all insist that God did alter His plans, so far by 2000 years, and that Jesus did fail to do what he came to do.

Fifth, as a result of disproving #4, we have shown how important it is to believe that God did not fail, that Jesus did not fail, and that the kingdom was established. If the views of these men, as well intentioned as they might be, are true, then the Bible is false.

Sixth, however, we have shown that God did keep His word, that Jesus did not fail, and that the Bible is trustworthy.

Seventh, we have shown how important it is to believe the right things about the last days and "time of the end." What we believe about the last days and the time of the end is important. It affects our politics. It affects our world, our nation, our lives.

We have spoken candidly about the false views of some very popular men. It is not our purpose to be caustic or offensive. However, much is at stake here. The credibility of Christianity is at stake. The trustworthiness of God is in question. The Deity of Jesus is being challenged, and the inspiration of scripture stands or falls on the validity of our last days beliefs. Sceptics continue to challenge believers with the very obviously failed predictions that the end will certainly be in our generation.

When will the modern church finally hold accountable the men who continue to bring shame on Christ's Word by their failed prophecies? History records a veritable parade of "prophecy experts" who pronounced that their calculations could not be wrong, that no other generation had ever had so much reason to believe the end was near. Yet, generation after generation, prophet after prophet has passed, and the anticipated end has not come. And the reason it has not come as they foretold is because they were prophesying the end of something, the Church Age, that the Bible says is *without end!* These false prophets have transferred to the church, the predictions made about the end of Israel's Age.

Virtually all scholars and Bible students will agree that the Bible speaks of eschatology in a vast number of passages. According to actual count, 2/3rds of the Bible, *that is once every 26 verses*, is concerned with eschatology, yet, eschatology is one of the most ignored Biblical topics, and considered by many to be a "non-issue." But if Jesus and his inspired apostles spoke and wrote about this topic so much, how can the modern church count it as a non-issue?

Paul stood trial and was willing to die for his view of the resurrection (Acts 23, 24, 26). Did Paul consider eschatology a non-issue? Some in his day were saying that the end of Israel's age had already occurred, but Paul said that in doing so, they were in violation of God's Word (Romans 11:1f). By the way, these folks were saying that Israel's last days, Israel's *eschaton*, had already come and gone, but Paul said they were wrong. This totally refutes the notion that God was through with Israel at the Cross. The point is, that in Romans 11 Paul was very concerned with eschatology, the end of the age, and he tied it directly to the end of *Israel's age,* when God would fulfill all of His promises to her.[72]

In light of the serious ramifications of saying that God's kingdom plan for Israel failed or was postponed, and in light of the overwhelming sense of the nearness of the end found in the New Testament,[73] it is time for the evangelical world to take a careful, analytical look at this topic.

This book is a call to action. It is a call to re-think. It is a call to study. It is a call to accountability. It is a call for the end of the sensational predictions that have no basis in fact, or in inspiration. It is a call to courage for speaking out against the abuse of God's word that is emanating from so many pulpits. It is a call for a New Reformation.[74] It is my fervent prayer and hope that the readers of this book will see the incredibly powerful truth that lies herein, and to see the marvelous Truth of God's Word. He told us when the last days were. He told us what He was going to do in the last days, *and He kept His word*. The last days are past, the future lies ahead, bright and hopeful. Let us march forward with confidence into a brighter day.

As I finished the major part of this book, John Anderson sent me an article written by Thomas Ice, whom we have cited often in this work. Ice seems to be the leading apologist for the dispensational camp at the time, and I have personally had three radio debates, and one formal public debate[75] with him. In the article Anderson sent to me, Ice addresses the issue of the "age to come." I thought it necessary to add here a special response and examination of Ice's article.

As we have noted, a cardinal doctrine of eschatology is that of "the age to come." The age to come was to be the time of the Messiah, the kingdom, and salvation. It was the anticipated goal of Israel's prophets. In the publication "Midnight Call," and an article entitled *The Age to Come,* Ice took issue with the preterist view *of the age to come* espoused by authors like Gary DeMar and myself. In that article, Ice set forth the dispensational objection to the view that *the age to come* arrived with the end of the Old Covenant Age of Israel in A.D. 70, and that Christians now live in, and enjoy the promised age to come.

We want first of all to set forth the Biblical view of *the age to come.* Let me remind the reader of three points made earlier:

1.) The Jews only believed in two ages. They believed in what they called "this age" and "the age to come."

2.) The Jews believed that *this age* was the age of Moses and the Law, and was, even as Ice suggests (p. 2), the time when Israel awaited the fulfillment of her prophetic hope. The Jews believed that *the age to come* would be the age of Messiah and the New Covenant. (cf. Hebrews 2:1-5).

3.) The Jews believed that *this age* would end, but the age of the Messiah*, the age to come*, would never end (Isaiah 9:6-9; Luke 1:32-33; Ephesians 3:20-21).

Jesus taught the existence of only two ages, and he used the terms *this age* and *the age to come.* He was living in *this age*, and anticipated *the age to come.* Thus, our **point #1 is established**. Ice concurs: "The Jewish perspective of Bible prophecy views history as consisting of two ages. The first was 'this present age,' the age in which Israel was waiting for the coming of Messiah. The second was 'the age to come,' the age in which all promises and covenants would be fulfilled and Israel would enter her promised blessings as a result of Messiah's coming." (p. 18).

The **second point** is also established in that Jesus definitely viewed his *this age* as the age of Moses and the Law. He was sent to establish the promises made to the fathers of Israel (Romans 15:6f). After all, Jesus was, "born of a woman, made under the Law" (Galatians 4:4). Also, Jesus was very aware of living under the age of Moses and the Law. He said he did not come to destroy it, but to fulfill it, and said it *all*, not *part*, not some, or not even *most* of it, *but all of it*, had to be fulfilled before it could pass (Matthew 5:17-18). We will return to this momentarily.

Jesus demonstrated the presence of *this age*, when the Mosaic mandates were still valid and binding, in his discussion with the Sadducees about resurrection. They appealed to the Levirate Marriage law of Deuteronomy, and Jesus concurred with its validity. However, he also anticipated the arrival of *the age to come* time when, "they neither marry nor are given in marriage" (Luke 20:35). This is not a description of the end of human relationships, as some mistakenly claim. It is a contrast between the Mosaic Age—founded, identified, and sustained by "marrying and giving in marriage," and *the age to come*, when members of the kingdom are determined, not by physical lineage, but by spiritual birth. Members of the kingdom today are not the result of marrying and giving in marriage. They are the result of being *taught*, and then being born into the kingdom (Hebrews 8:6f).

The point is that for Jesus, *this age* was indeed the age of Moses and the Law, and *the age to come* was the age when Moses and the Law would no longer be binding.

Our **third point** is established by the Olivet Discourse. Jesus predicted the destruction of the Temple (Matthew 23-24:2). The disciples associated the desolation of that edifice with the end of the age (*sunteliea ton aionion*) and asked for a sign, "of the end of the age." It is common for modern commentators to claim, even as Ice *seems* to do, that the disciples *mistakenly* associated the destruction of that Temple with the end of the age. It is even sometimes claimed that the disciples could not conceive of the Temple's destruction in any other context than the end of time and the destruction of creation. Of course, this is a false claim. The disciples knew the Temple was destroyed in B. C. 586 did they not? Well, if they knew the Temple was destroyed in B. C. 586, and yet time did not end and the earth was not destroyed, why should we think that is what they were thinking of when Jesus said the Temple was to be destroyed again?

The disciples clearly did associate the end of the age with the destruction of the Temple *that was standing when they asked the question.* Ice admits that Jesus' prediction prompted the disciples to think of Zechariah 14:[76] "The disciples, who were questioning Jesus on the Mount of Olives, linked Christ's words of judgment about the destruction of the present Temple with the invasion of Jerusalem that was predicted by Zechariah." (*Call*, 18).

Well, if Jesus' prediction of the destruction of the Temple *that was standing when they were alive*, 2000 years ago, caused them to think of Zechariah 14 the disciples were either right or wrong to make that association. Of course, Ice believes they were wrong, because in his view, Zechariah 14 could not have been fulfilled in the destruction of A.D. 70. But, if they were wrong, just where did Jesus correct them? Where did he say, "You foolish and slow to learn"? or, "You do not know the scriptures"? He made no such statements. If the disciples were right to associate the destruction of the *then standing Temple* with the end of the age, millennialism is nullified. To show that the disciples were not mistaken, we turn to Daniel 12

Daniel was given a vision of the time of the end (Daniel 12: 4, 9-10). The predictions included the forecast of the time of tribulation (v. 1), and the abomination of desolation (v. 9f). One angel asked another angel when these things would be fulfilled, when the time of the end would be (v. 6). The answer from heaven was: "When the power of the holy people is completely shattered all these things will be fulfilled (v. 7)." Thus, according to Daniel 12, the time when Israel's power would be completely shattered would be the end of the age.[77] What was Israel's power? It was the Temple, the priesthood, the Feast days, her *Law*, and everything that those things stood for. When was that power destroyed? It was in A.D. 70.

So, Daniel 12 proves that the end of the age is tied inseparably to the destruction of Israel. The disciples were not confused, nor were they ignorant therefore, when they connected Jesus' prediction of the Temple's demise to the end of the age. They were asking a perfectly legitimate and logical question based on their knowledge of the prophetic scriptures.

Furthermore, we know that the disciples were not confused about the end of the age, and Daniel's prediction, *because they specifically tell us so*! In Matthew 13:31f, Jesus told the parable of the wheat and the tares. He says that at the end of "*this age*" the Son would send forth the angels and they would gather the elect (v. 39-40). Ice even admits that in Matthew 13:39 Jesus, "continued to speak within the contemporary Jewish framework." (*Call*, p. 18).

This is a *huge* admission. Ice says that in Matthew 13 Jesus was using the term *this age* within the contemporary Jewish framework. In other words, his use of *this age, and "the end of this age," were made within the context of Jewish understanding.* This means that Jesus' referent to *this age* has to be to *the then present Age of Israel*. However, *in reality*, Ice believes that: "The parables of Matthew 13 provide insight into the course of *the current Church Age.* (My emphasis, DKP) Actually, since Matthew 13 surveys this present age in its relationship to the kingdom, the parables cover the period of time between Christ's two advents—His first and second comings." (*Prophecy*, 44) But this will not do.

Remember that in Matthew 13 Jesus is quoting Daniel 12, and its prediction of the end of the age. It is critical to know that the dispensationalists does not believe that the church or the Church Age is predicted anywhere in the Old Testament. To the millennialists, the church was a totally unrevealed mystery in the O.T. If the Old Testament does not predict the Church Age, then it is certain that the Old Testament does not predict *the end of the Church Age!* However, Ice says that Matthew 13 is predictive of the end of "the current Christian Age." Since Matthew 13 is about the fulfillment of Daniel 12, *then if it is about the end of the current Christian Age as Ice claims*, this totally refutes the millennial contention that the Old Testament does not mention the Church Age!

Ice cannot have it both ways. He cannot maintain his position that the Old Testament does not predict anything about the Church Age, since Matthew 13 is about the fulfillment of Daniel 12. Yet, Ice claims that Matthew 13 is predictive of the end of the Church Age. However, if he concurs that Matthew 13 is about the end of the age as contemporary Jewish usage had it, then it cannot be maintained that Matthew 13 is about the end of the Christian Age. The Jews had no concept, or belief about the end of the Christian Age!

Jesus said the end of the age he was predicting in Matthew 13 *would be the fulfillment of Old Testament prophecy.* This can only mean that he was predicting the end of *Israel's Old Covenant Age.* This means that Matthew 13 has no connection with the Rapture, which supposedly brings the *Church Age* to an end.[78]

So, per Ice, although Jesus was using the terms *this age* and *end of the age* in the accepted and normally understood Jewish manner, and gave no indication he was referring to anything else, in truth, he was not referring to anything remotely related to the fulfillment of Israel's promises and prophecies!

In Matthew 13 Jesus used the identical distinctive term for the end of the age that the disciples used in Matthew 24:3 (*suntelia tou aionos*). In verse 43, Jesus said that at the end of his "this age," "the righteous shall shine forth," a direct quote of Daniel 12:3. By the way, it is fascinating that Ice believes that Matthew 13 is about the end of "the current Christian Age," but he believes that Matthew 24:3, and the Olivet Discourse, "Is given to Israel—not the church" (*Fast*, 145) This in spite of the fact that Matthew 13 and Matthew 24 *use the identical Greek term* for end of the age, both use the identical language to describe that event, and both say that Old Testament prophecy would be fulfilled in the events being foretold.

Daniel predicted the end of the age, when Israel's promises would be fulfilled. He said the end of his *this age*, would be, "when the power of the holy people is completely shattered" (Daniel 12:4-7). Jesus, in Matthew 13, told a parable about the end of his *this age,* and said it would occur when Daniel 12 was fulfilled! In other words, Daniel predicted that Israel's *this age* would end with the judgment on Israel! Remember, this is what we saw in Genesis 49 as well. The correlation is beautiful. Now watch closely.

Jesus proceeded to tell two other parables about the end of the age, and used the identical distinctive Greek term for end of the age (v. 49), that he used in v. 39-40. He then pointedly asked his disciples, "Have you understood these things?" (v. 51). According to most dispensationalists, the idea of a link between the time of judgment on Israel and the end of the age is misguided. However, the disciples did not hesitate. They said "Yes." *Were they lying?*

So, what we have is this, Jesus told a parable about the end of Israel's *this age*, and said the end of the age, would be fulfilled when Daniel 12 was fulfilled. However, Daniel said the end of the age would come, "when the power of the holy people has been completely shattered" (Daniel 12:7). Jesus asked his disciples if they understood what he was teaching them about the end of the age as foretold by Daniel, and they said, *"Yes."* Then, in Matthew 24, Jesus predicted the destruction of the Temple, *the epitome and symbol of the power of Israel.* The disciples, upon hearing of the impending judgment of that *then standing Temple*, immediately asked for a sign of the end of the age. They used the identical Greek term used by Jesus in his discussion of the fulfillment of Daniel's prediction of the end of the age—*the discussion they said they understood.* Yet, we are supposed to think that now, in Matthew, the disciples were wrong to link the judgment of that then standing Temple with the end of the age. We are supposed to believe that they were confused. It is evident, however, that the disciples were not the ones confused. It is those today who refuse to make the same connection that they did between the end of the age and the judgment on Israel that are confused.

After all, what age would end with the destruction of the Temple? *What age did the Temple epitomize and symbolize?* It assuredly did not represent the Christian Age! Was it not Jesus' *this age*, the Mosaic Age? And, if *this age* was to end with the fall of Jerusalem, then does it not follow that *the age to come* would arrive with the end of *this age*?

Not only would Jesus' *this age* end with the destruction of the Temple, *the age to come, would never end.* In Matthew 24:35 Jesus said, "Heaven and earth shall pass away, but my word shall never pass away." While most people try to make this a prediction of the passing of literal creation, it is better to understand it in the historical context in which it is given. Jesus was discussing the end of *this age*, when the Temple was destroyed. What is important to realize is that the Temple was called "heaven and earth" by the Jews of Jesus' day!

Josephus, the contemporary of Paul described the Temple and says the Most Holy Place was called *heaven,* and that the Holy Place was called *earth and sea.*[79] Thus, it was perfectly natural for Jesus, as he described the destruction of that wonderful edifice, to say "heaven and earth shall pass." However, he also said, "but my word shall never pass away." Here, in one verse, we have the contrast between the two ages! The *this age* of Jesus, symbolized by the Temple, was going to pass in that generation (v. 34), and *the age to come,* the age of Jesus the Messiah, would be established and never pass away!

So, we have proven our three points above. The Jews believed in only two ages. Those two ages were the age of Moses and the Law, and the Age of Messiah and the New Covenant. The Age of Moses was to end, but the age of Messiah was not to end. Let's take a look now at the millennial view posited by Ice.

THE CHURCH AGE IS NOW *THIS AGE*, REPLACING ISRAEL'S *THIS AGE?*

If it is true that Jesus' *this age* was the age of Israel, the age of Moses and the Law, as Ice admits, this means that the Old Law would not end until *the age to come* arrived. Biblically, *the age to come* would arrive only when the Old Law passed away, and Israel's law would only pass when it was completely fulfilled. Take a look at Matthew 5:17-18:

"Do not think that I am come to destroy the Law and the Prophets, I am not come to destroy, but to fulfill. For verily I say unto you, until heaven and earth passes away, not one jot or one tittle shall pass from the Law until it is all fulfilled."

The Old Testament would stand valid until Israel received her promises. (See Hebrews 9:6-10). You cannot, as Ice and others attempt to do, delineate between the Mosaic Covenant and the promises made to Israel. You cannot say the Mosaic Covenant has been completely fulfilled and removed in Christ, and then, as Ice does, appeal to the Mosaic Covenant for prophecies of the restoration of Israel in 1948, and a yet future restoration![80]

Israel's *this age* would remain valid until it gave way to *the age to come.* Ice says this was the common Jewish use of the term. However, he also says, "I believe that 'this present age' refers to the current Church Age that began almost 2000 years ago on the day of Pentecost when the Church was founded." (*Call*, 1). This means that Israel's *this age* was postponed, at Pentecost, and that another *this age* replaced Israel's *this age*, in anticipation of the ultimate restoration of Israel's *this age*, which of course, will then give way to the real *"age to come!"* Did you catch that?

It is abundantly ironic that the paradigm that resists what they call "Replacement Theology" is so adamant about proclaiming Replacement Theology! Israel's *this age* has been replaced by *this age* of the church. Israel's promises have been replaced by the promises of the body of Christ. The Bride of Christ has replaced Israel in the eye of Jehovah. The Law has been replaced by the Gospel of Grace.

Where is the transition from Israel's *this age*, to the church as *this age?* Where do the inspired writers say that the Church Age has temporarily taken the place of Israel's age, to await a yet future reinstatement of Israel's *this age*? On the contrary, Ice tells us that Paul, "continues to use the phrases *'this age'* and *'the age to come'* in the way that Christ used them." (*Call*, 18). Okay, if Jesus used the terms *this age*, and *the age to come* in the established Jewish manner, and Paul continued to use the terms *that same way*, then how in the world can Ice claim that Paul, "Viewed the current Church Age as the time leading up to the coming of Messiah, thus, we are still in 'this age." Notice the quandary created by Ice's view.

Ice claims that the Church Age is now the *this age* of Paul and the New Testament writers. He even says "There is an urgency concerning the entire Church Age in which we now live. For example, Paul, speaking of the entire Church Age, calls it 'the present distress' (1 Corinthians 7:26)" (*Call*, 19). There is a major problem here!

What did Paul have to say about "the present distress?" He said, "It is good for a man to remain as he is...are you loosed from a wife? Do not seek a wife." (1 Corinthians 7:26-27). In other words, because of the "present distress," which Ice claims *is the entirety of the Christian Age*, Paul said it is better for man not to marry! Has Ice begun to proclaim celibacy? If not, why not? Paul was assuredly counseling celibacy, as a direct result of "the present distress."

For Paul, "the present distress" was not an extended age of so far 2000 years. It was *his generation* when, "The end of the ages has come upon us," (10:11), and ,"the time has been shortened... the form of this world is passing away" (1 Corinthians 7:29,31). Ice has completely ignored, or distorted, the urgency of the context. He has ignored the fact that Paul urged celibacy in light of the "present distress." It is illogical for Ice to claim that the Church Age is Paul's "the present distress," and then to ignore Paul's mandates of how to live in "the present distress."

The reader might not have caught the subtlety of Ice's transition, from Israel's *this age*, to the church as *this age*, nor how destructive this is to his view. A fundamental doctrine of dispensationalism is the distinction between Israel and the church. We are told that the promises of Israel are totally distinct from the church: "The church is unique in the plan of God and separate from His plan for Israel." (*Fast*, 43)

But wait! Ice has Israel's *this age*, wholly identified now with the *this age* of the church! Paul, remember, used the terms *this age* and *the age to come* in the same way Jesus did. However, Jesus used the terms in the Jewish context of his contemporaries, as a reference to the age of Israel—not the Church Age! Paul used the terms the same way, Ice affirms, but, and this is huge, Paul actually is using the terms to speak of the Church Age which is in no way related to the Age of Israel. Ice has wedded Israel's *this age* terminology to *this age* of the Church, and hoped no one would notice.

If Paul was using the term *this age* in the same way Jesus used the terms, and if Jesus used the terms to speak of *Israel's this age*, distinctive from the church, then it is patently obvious that Paul was using the term to speak of *Israel's this age*. It must be remembered that Paul repeatedly stated that he preached nothing but the hope of Israel. His gospel was the fulfillment of God's promises to Abraham (Acts 24:14f; 26:9f; 28:18f). Paul was not writing about *this age, the age to come*, *the end of the age* and *the age to come* isolated and distinct from the promises made to Israel.   This being true, to say that *this age* was, or is, still present is to say that the Old Law is still valid. Remember, Jesus said *none of the Old Covenant*, and that means his *this age*, would pass until it was all fulfilled. Thus, for Ice and the dispensationalists to say that *this age* is still present is to *demand* that the Old Law, *all of it*, remains valid. It will not do to say that the Church Age, distinct from Israel's *this age*, is now the present age. Jesus' words are not open to dispute. He said that not one iota of the Old Covenant, and thus *his this age*, would pass, until it was all fulfilled. But the time of the fulfillment of Israel's Old Covenant would be the arrival of *the age to come*!

Another point to ponder. If Paul used the term this age to refer to the Christian Age, *then the Jewish leaders are "the rulers of this age!* Paul said "the rulers of this age" were the ones responsible for killing Jesus " (1 Corinthians 2:6f). Who killed Jesus? You can equivocate all you wish, but it was the Jews who said, "Let his blood be on us and on our children!" (Matthew 27:25). Thus, if *this age* refers to the Christian Age in Paul's writings, then the Jewish leaders are the rulers of the Christian Age! Do we really want to take a position that says that the rulers of the nation that hated, reviled, and killed the "Lord of Glory" are in fact, the rulers of the age that he died to establish? I thought *Jesus* was the ruler of the Christian Age!

> **If "this age" is the Christian Age, then the Jewish leaders who killed Jesus are the rulers of the Christian Age, because Paul said it was the rulers of "this age" that killed Jesus!**

There is another huge problem with Ice's claim that Paul's use of *this age* displaced the Jewish *this age*, and that his *this age* is now the Church Age. Ice says (*Call*, 18), that in Galatians 1:4 Paul is referring to the Church Age. Read the text carefully: "Who (Jesus, DKP), gave Himself for our sins, that He might deliver us from this present evil age, according to the will of our God and Father." You just have to catch the power of the problem Ice has created for himself.

Paul said Christ died to save us from "this present evil age." However, per Ice, *this present age is the Church Age*. Therefore, Jesus died to deliver Christians from the Church Age! Do you see the problem? Did Jesus die to deliver Christians from the very Age, that he died to establish? Remember, Jesus came to establish the Church Age by his death. Even Ice and LaHaye admit this! See their comments above. So, on the one hand, Jesus died *to establish the Church Age*, the Age of Grace, but, according to Ice, Jesus actually died *to deliver us from the Christian Age*, because it is "evil!" By the way, just how can Ice claim that Paul calls the Christian Age, this age, and call it the Age of Grace and forgiveness, and then claim that Paul is referring to the current Christian Age as "evil?"

THE AGE OF ISRAEL, MOSES AND THE LAW?

As we have seen, Ice says that God terminated the Mosaic Law, and has now substituted the church, an unknown and un-prophesied mystery, as *this age*. Thus, Jesus' *this age*, the Age of Moses and the Law, has now given way to the church as *this age*. One thing this posit does is to delineate between the Mosaic Age and the Age of Israel. It says that God could bring an end to the Age of Moses and the Law, while still maintaining the existence at some point, of the Age of Israel. You see, Ice says that God ended the Mosaic Age of the Law, *forever*, and in so doing, simply postponed Israel's *this age* until some point in the future after the rapture of the church when the 70th Week of Daniel will resume its countdown.

This view tacitly identifies the age of Moses and the Law as the Age of Israel, but then, of necessity, divorces *the Age of Israel from the Age of Moses and the Law*, and preserves and projects the Age of Israel into the future. It says that God could end the Age of Moses, *but not the Age of Israel!* This is artificial to say the very least. Even Ice admits that *this age* was the age in which Israel looked for her Messiah (*Call*, 18). Well, was Israel longing for and looking for the Messiah under Moses and the Law? If so, then the Age of Moses and the Law was indeed Israel's this age, and *the age to come* was to be the age that would arrive with the consummation of the Age of Moses and the Law. This is none other than the Christian Age.

THE MYSTERY OF THE CHURCH:
KNOWN OR UNKNOWN?

One of the essential tenets of the dispensational paradigm is the idea that the church was not predicted by the Old Testament prophets:

> "The concept must stand that this whole age with its program was not revealed in the Old Testament, but constitutes a new program and a new line of revelation in this present age....It has been illustrated how this whole age existed in the mind of God without having been revealed in the Old Testament." (Pentecost, 137)

Ice concurs: "The church was an unrevealed mystery, which is why it began suddenly, without warning, and why this age will end suddenly and mysteriously at the rapture." (*Fast Facts*, p. 43) Speaking of the Church Age, Spargimino says, "The Hebrew prophets knew nothing of this phase," of God's plan.(*Anti-Prophets*, 195)

If it can be shown that the church was predicted by the Old Covenant prophets, and we have done that already, then, in reality, the entire millennial world collapses, for this means that the Church Age is indeed the age to come that Israel was anticipating.

Before moving on to that however, we need to take note that the millennialists actually contradict themselves in regard to whether the church was predicted by the Old Testament prophets or not. Note that Ice claims that the church was an unknown, unrevealed mystery. However, when Jesus read from Isaiah 61 (Luke 4:18), about the proclamation of the "acceptable year of the Lord," Ice and LaHaye claim: "That's a reference to the Church Age, often called the age of grace." *(Charting, 30)*

So, on the one hand, the church is an *unrevealed mystery, unknown to the Old Testament prophets*, but on the other hand, *Isaiah 61 foretold the Church Age!* If Isaiah 61 *foretold the Church Age*, then pretty clearly, it is wrong to say the church was an unrevealed, unknown mystery. That is a serious contradiction. But this is not all.

Ice and LaHaye demonstrate confusion and contradiction about why Jesus came. On the one hand, they claim he came to establish the kingdom, but of course, that offer was rejected and the kingdom was postponed. However, what is not often known, is that these "prophecy experts" *also deny that Jesus came to establish the kingdom!* Notice: "The purpose of his first coming was to announce the period of grace and salvation we are living in, not the time of judgment that is yet to come." (*Charting*, 30) So, Jesus did not come to establish the kingdom after all, even though when Ice debated Gentry, he claimed that Jesus did come to establish the kingdom, and it was only the Jewish rejection that prevented that from happening. But here is the point.

Per Ice, Jesus did not come to establish the kingdom, he came to proclaim the church, the age of grace. However, Jesus said he came to suffer, and *the purpose of his suffering was to purchase the church* (Acts 20:28). However, if Jesus came to suffer and thereby establish the church, then since the Old Testament predicted his *suffering* (Psalms 22, 22; Isaiah 53, etc.), it is manifest that *the Old Testament did foretell the church*. You cannot say that the OT did not predict the establishment of the church, and then say that it did predict Jesus' suffering, *which was to establish the church. The prediction of his suffering was the prediction of the church!*

Joel 2-3 is one of the most important passages of appeal to the millennialists. It is claimed that in these two great chapters the prophet spoke of the fulfillment of Israel's salvation kingdom promises. This is true of course, but the problem is, the New Testament writers affirm that Joel was fulfilled in the body of Christ!

On the day of Pentecost, (Acts 2), the apostles were gathered together. They received the outpouring of the Spirit, and spoke in tongues. When accused of being drunk, Peter responded, "Ye men of Israel, hear these words, for these men are not drunk as you suppose, since it is but the third hour of the day, but, this is that which was spoken by the prophet Joel." Peter then quotes, verbatim, the prophecy of Joel 2:28-30.

The millennialists, remember, say that Joel could not be speaking of the church, for the church is never predicted in the Old Testament. Joel had to be speaking of the last days of Israel and the fulfillment of her Messianic promises. Ice says that what happened on Pentecost was the establishment of the church and the *this age* of the church, which has temporarily displaced Israel's *this age*. The trouble for Ice is that he, and dispensationalism as a whole, *is at direct odds with the inspired text.*

Note that Peter said, "this is that which was spoken by the prophet Joel." Now, ask yourself: How much clearer could this be? If Peter wanted to tell his audience that what they were seeing was the fulfillment of Joel, would the words "this is that" convey that message? Further, if Peter did not think it was the fulfillment of Joel, in fact bearing *virtually no resemblance* to Joel's prophecy, why even bring up the prophecy of Joel? And, if you would have been standing there, and had seen those events, when Peter said, "This is that which was spoken by the prophet Joel," would you have thought he was in fact saying, "Virtually nothing that has happened here this day was predicted by Joel"? Would you have taken his "This is that," to mean, This is not that"?

Ice believes that, "Virtually nothing that happened in Acts 2 is predicted in Joel 2."[81] Well, let's see, Joel said the Spirit was to be poured out, and *the Spirit was poured out.* Joel said the Spirit was to be poured out in miraculous manner. The Spirit was poured out in miraculous manner. Joel said the Spirit was to be poured out on Israel. The Spirit was poured out, and offered to, the house of Israel. Joel said that when the Spirit was poured out on Israel that the remnant of Israel, and all men, could then be saved, and Peter offered his audience "the remission of sins," i.e. salvation. Joel said what would happen in the last days, and Peter said, "This is that which was spoken by the prophet Joel!" Yet, we are to believe that "virtually nothing" that happened on Pentecost was foretold by Joel!

It is claimed that Acts 2 could not be the fulfillment of Joel, because, "Joel was speaking of the out pouring of the Spirit on the nation of Israel in the last days." This is *circular reasoning*. It says the events of Pentecost could not be the fulfillment of Joel. How do we know? Because Joel was to be fulfilled in the last days of Israel, and the last days of Israel did not exist on Pentecost. Therefore, the events of Acts 2 were not the fulfillment of Joel. See how that works? It sounds good, but proves nothing.

In other words, even though Peter *was inspired by the Holy Spirit* to say, "This is that which was spoken by the prophet Joel," it could not have been what Joel predicted, because Ice and his compatriots do not believe the last days of Israel existed on Pentecost. Dispensationalists claim to know the prophecies better than the inspired apostle Peter! The logic is circular, and it is called *petitio principii*. It begs the question. It assumes a view to be true because they say it is true, not because the text says so.

Where is the literalism that Ice and the millennialists say is the only true guiding principle to Biblical interpretation? How can they claim they interpret the Bible literally when they take Peter's statement, "This is that which was spoken by the prophet Joel" and turn it into, "This is *not* that which was spoken by the prophet Joel"? The millennial denial of Peter's words identify the millennialists as *Disciples of Denial*.[82]

Unless Peter was mistaken, the events of Acts 2 were the fulfillment of Joel's prophecy.[83] Since what occurred on Pentecost was *the establishment of the church*, two important facts come to mind.

First, the millennial contention that the Old Testament did not predict the church is falsified. Patently, if what Joel predicted was being fulfilled on Pentecost, and if what was happening on Pentecost was the establishment of the *church*, it is wrong to say the Old Testament did not predict the church.

Second, if Acts 2 was the fulfillment of Joel 2, then it is abundantly clear that the church is the fulfillment of Israel's Messianic promises. And this means that Israel's *this age* was coming to an end even as *the age to come* was breaking into the Old Aeon. This is the perfect, logical explanation for why Paul and the rest of the New Testament authors continued to use the terms *this age* and *age to come* in the normal manner without changing or modifying the usage at all. They understood that they were living in the last days of *this age*, and that its end was near. *The age to come was near!*

IS THE CHURCH AGE TEMPORARY?

Now, if it is true that the church was predicted by the Old Testament prophets then the idea that the church has displaced the Mosaic Age as *this age* is falsified, and, in fact, *the Church Age is demonstrated to be the age to come!* Even Ice admits that the Mosaic *this age* ended and gave way to the church. Well, this means that from the perspective of the Old Law, *the Church Age was the age to come.* It not only means that the Church Age is the anticipated age to come, but it means that the Church Age has no end.

It is essential to the millennial view that the Church Age come to an end. (Of course, it is also imperative for the amillennial and postmillennial views as well, but we will not go into that here.) Ice even makes the totally unfounded claim that: "Three New Testament passages (Romans 16:25-27; Ephesians 3:1-13; Colossians 2:4-3:3) teach that the Church Age is a temporary mystery in God's overall plan." *(Call, 19).*

Romans 16:25-26 says not one thing about the temporary nature of the church or the temporary proclamation of the Gospel. It does say that Paul was, "by the scriptures of the prophets, according to the commandment of the everlasting God" making known the mystery of the Gospel. Now here is something to ponder. If the Church Age was totally unknown, *and is not contained in the Old Covenant Scriptures*, how in the world could Paul and the early church be making the mystery known "by the scriptures of the prophets"? How could Paul reveal the mystery from the Old Testament if the Old Testament never mentions the church?

In Ephesians 3, the same apostle has not one thing to say about the temporary nature of the church. He simply says that he was given the task of making the mystery of God known. By the way, here is an important point. Paul does not say that the *Church* was an unknown, unpredicted mystery. He says that it was *Jew and Gentile equality in the Church* that was the mystery that was not understood in previous times, "as it is now revealed unto the sons of men." You see, the Old Testament definitely taught of Gentiles being brought into the kingdom (Isaiah 49), but the *full equality* between Jew and Gentile in the kingdom was not fully explicated. That is the mystery. The Church was not a mystery.

Colossians says *nothing* about the temporary nature of the church. There is not one word about the church enduring until Israel is re-established. There *is,* however, a discourse on the world of Israel being done away, however (Colossians 2:20). There is *not one word* about the end of the Church Age! There *is* the teaching that in Christ, believers are God's *New Creation*, and this is what the Old Testament anticipated (Isaiah 65).

Rather than teaching that the Church Age is temporary, by calling attention to the fact that the Church is what the Old Covenant prophecies anticipated, the writer was establishing the unending nature of the Church. The New Creation, per Paul *the Church* (2 Corinthians 5:15; Ephesians 2:15f, 4:23f; Colossians 3:9f, etc.), would stand forever and never pass away (Isaiah 66:19f).

The passages adduced by Ice to prove the temporary nature of the Church Age prove just the opposite. This is not really surprising since I have discovered that Ice is more than willing to cite passages as supportive of his view that are in fact, *total refutations of his positions*! Not only do these passages not support the idea of a temporary Church Age, Paul and the New Testament authors are emphatic that the Church Age has no end.

Notice that in Ephesians 1:10 Paul says that it was *God's eternal purpose* to reunite heaven and earth in the one body of Christ, and to do this in *the fullness of time*. Jesus appeared in the fullness of time (Galatians 4:4). Thus, unless Jesus failed, as the millennial paradigm seems all too willing to affirm, then the first century was the time for the summing up of all things in Christ. It would seem to go without saying, by the way, that if this work of reconciliation was the eternal purpose of God that it is totally inappropriate to speak of it as an unanticipated, unexpected, and unwanted "Plan B" in the Scheme of God!

Further, notice that Paul in Ephesians 3:21 says, "Unto Him be glory in the Church, by Jesus Christ, throughout all ages, world without end, Amen!" Paul affirms that the Church Age is unending! This means that the Church Age was/is *the age to come* anticipated by Israel's prophets.

Paul affirmed the same thing of the Church in Hebrews 12. He reminded his readers that their salvation did not lie in the old things of Israel, but in the realities of Christ. He told them that Israel's Age was only a shadow of better things that about to come at "the time of reformation" (Hebrews 9:10). This time of *reformation* (Greek, *diorthosis*), is the time of Israel's salvation according to the OT prophets (Isaiah 62:7, LXX). In other words, Israel's *this age* was to endure until *the age to come*. He told them that they were even then, "receiving a kingdom that cannot be shaken" (Hebrews 12:28). *That kingdom they were receiving was the church* (12:21f) The Church, *and thus the Church Age*, is unshakable, unmovable. It is eternal!

It is important to note that the Hebrew writer sets forth the Church as the fulfillment of the Old Covenant promises of God's eternal blessings in

Zion. Hebrews 12 hearkens back to many Old Covenant promises, but Isaiah 24-25 are in the background. In that prophecy, God would destroy Israel, break the curse of the sin and death, and rule in Zion. In Hebrews, the author says, "You have come to Mt. Zion, the City of the Living God!" For the author to affirm that his Jewish readers were coming to the promised blessings of Zion is the strongest of statements that *the age to come* was on them!

Ice and the millennialists must have a temporary Church Age for their views to stand. Yet, the New Testament authors repeatedly say the Church will never pass away. Since the Jews believed that only the Mosaic Covenant would end, and that the Kingdom of Messiah—*the age to come*-- would never end, and since the Bible affirms that the Church Age that followed the passing of the Mosaic Age *will never end*, then it must be true that the Church Age is the promised *age to come.*

THE END OF THE AGES HAS COME UPON US!

What we have shown is consistent with the NT testimony that the end of the age was near, and that the New Creation was about to be fully revealed. If Ice's posit is true, that the Church Age was substituted for Israel's *this age,* there is no way that all of the New Testament references to the soon coming realization of Israel's promises was near could have been true. Yet, this is precisely what we find.

Not only did Paul say that the goal of the previous ages was about to arrive, Peter said, "the end of all things has drawn near" (1 Peter 4:7), and John wrote, "Little children it is the last hour. As you have heard that anti-christ should come, even now there are many anti-christs, thereby you know it is the last hour" (1 John 2:18). In the Apocalypse, John was told that the mystery of God foretold by all the prophets was about to be fulfilled, and there was not going to be any further delay (Revelation 10:7f), the time was "at hand."

These emphatic time indicators, taken in context of the *this age* versus *the age to come* discussion, take on extra meaning. Are we to believe that Paul, James, John and Peter began saying the end of the Church Age was near, within just a few short years of its establishment? Are we to suppose that the eternal purpose of God, in the Church purchased with the blood of Christ, was destined to be replaced so soon after its establishment? How could the New Testament writers predict the end of the Church Age, when in fact they repeatedly say *the Church Age will never end?*

It is significant that Ice completely ignores all references to the nearness of the end of the age in the first century. To give those passages credence is to renounce millennialism. You cannot honor the many NT time statements that the end of the age was near in the first century, and maintain the view of *this age*, and the *age to come* posited by Ice.

Summary: We have shown that the doctrine of *this age* and *the age to come* espoused by Ice is fundamentally flawed. His position is both confused and confusing, but worse, is at total odds with the scriptures

Ice says that Jesus and Paul used the terms *this age*, and *the age to come*, in the commonly accepted Jewish manner to speak of the Age of Israel and the Messianic Age. However, in reality, Paul affixed a *totally different* meaning to the terms. Whereas Jesus used the term *this age*, to speak of the Age of Israel anticipating the arrival of the Messianic Kingdom, Paul, *without indicating any change in his application of the terms*, used the term *this age* to speak of the current Church Age. The problem is that to the millennialists, there should be no application of *this age* to the Church Age because the promises of *this age* belong strictly to Israel and not the Church!

Ice subtly creates *two Old Covenant Ages*, the Age of Moses and the Law, which he says is ended forever, and the Age of Israel, which he insists is yet future.

He asserts the end of the endless Christian Age, and substitutes the Church Age for Israel's *this age*, something most millennialists are loathe to do. We have shown that the Church Age is endless.

Ice says the Church Age was not foretold in the Old Testament, and yet, Peter said the establishment of the church on Pentecost was the fulfillment of a key Messianic text of the Old Covenant, Joel 2. Further, Paul said his proclamation of the mystery of God was grounded in the Old Testament prophetic scriptures. If the Old Testament did not predict the mystery of God, or the Church, Paul could hardly preach that doctrine, correctly, from the OT.

We have shown that Ice's views are fatally flawed. He contradicts his own statements, but, most importantly, his views contradict the inspired Word of God. There is no Biblical merit to Ice's bold claims. Ice has slipped again.

END NOTES

1. Interestingly, Tim LaHaye and Thomas Ice have written a new book, entitled *The End Times Controversy: The Second Coming Under Attack.* (Eugene, Ore., Harvest House). The purpose of the book is to negate the position taken in this and other preterist books. However, in their book of well over 450+ pages, *the identity of the last days is never even discussed!* (Ice does address the 70 Weeks of Daniel but the specific issue of the last days is ignored). Their position is simply taken for granted. However, the definition of the last days as set forth in this book is a total refutation of *End Times Controversy.*

2. Kenneth Gentry, *He Shall Have Dominion*, Tyler, Tx. Institute for Christian Economics, 1992)328

3. See Thomas Ice and Timothy Demy's, *Prophecy Watch*, (Eugene, Ore., Harvest House, 1998)9+

4. The Sanhedrin as recorded in the Babylonian Talmud, ch. 4, folio 37.

5. For instance, the Romans granted Israel the right to kill anyone violating the sanctity of the Temple. There were inscriptions posted at intervals along the wall surrounding the Court of Israel, warning Gentiles that entrance beyond that point would lead to their death.

6. See my book, *Who Is This Babylon?* for a full discussion of Israel filling the measure of her sin by persecuting the saints.

7. In my audio book, *Jesus' Coming: In the Glory of the Father*, I show conclusively that the popular modern view that national Israel remains as God's determinative purpose is wrong. Old Covenant Israel was a mere shadow of God's ultimate purpose, the blood bought church of the Lord.

8. Charles Spurgeon, *Metropolitan Tabernacle Pulpit*, quoted by John Bray, *The New Heaven and the New Earth*, (Lakeland, Fl. John Bray Ministry)26. Thanks to John Anderson for pointing me to the quotation.

9. Tim LaHaye and Thomas Ice, *Charting the End Times*, (Eugene, Ore, 2001)27

10. N. T. Wright, *Jesus and the Victory of God*, (Minneapolis, Fortress, 1996)498

11. *The Bible Knowledge Commentary*, John Walvoord and Roy Zuck, (Wheaton, Ill., Victor Books, 1984)70. It is incredible that Walvoord says the parable actually suggests that the kingdom was only being taken from *that generation of Israel*, but that it will one day be restored to her once again. He refuses to acknowledge that the "other nation" suggests the Gentiles. To Walvoord, the *other nation*, simply means a *different generation of Israel.*

12. Donald Hagner, *Word Biblical Commentary, Matthew 14-28*, Vol. 33b (Dallas, Word, 1995)630

13. It is impossible to delineate between the Mosaic kingdom and the Davidic kingdom. What covenant did David operate under? What covenant did he live and rule by? Thus, while millennialists like to say the Davidic kingdom will be restored, but the Mosaic Covenant will not be restored, this ignores the reality of history. If the Davidic kingdom is to truly be restored as it was, then the Mosaic Covenant has to be restored as well.

14. A great deal more could be said about *diorthosis*, especially in regard to Acts 3:21f, and another key word *apokatastasis*, which means to restore, as *diorthosis*. I develop the significance of these two words in relationship to each other in my first affirmative speech in a public debate held in Queens, New York, April of 2002. The tapes of that debate are available from our website www.eschatology.org.

15. See my audio book *Jesus' Coming: In the Glory of the Father*, for a full discussion of the fact that Old Covenant national Israel, was a shadow of better thing to come, i.e. the spiritual body of Christ. One of the greatest theological tragedies of all time is the view that Old Covenant national Israel is of higher value in the eyes of God than the blood bought institute of the church, and that the church will one day be replaced by national Israel. It was ever and always God's eternal plan that the Old Covenant form of Israel would pass when she had fulfilled her purpose to bring in the Messiah. The book is available from our website: www.eschatology.org.

16. It needs to be understood that at the time of Isaiah's prediction, the 10 Northern tribes had already been cut off from David (2 Kings 17:20f), and had been *destroyed never to*

rise again nationally (Hosea 1:4, Amos 5:1-2). When Jesus said, "the kingdom would be taken from you" he was referring directly to Genesis 49. The restoration of Israel, promised by the prophets, was to be the engrafting of the remnant as promised by Hosea 1:10-11. Paul and Peter both affirm that this was being accomplished in Christ, in the church. This is powerful testimony as to the nature of the restoration of Israel.

17. George Peter Holford, *The Destruction of Jerusalem, An Absolute and Irresistible Proof of the Divine Origin of Christianity*, (Nacogdoches, TX., Covenant Media Press, 2001 reprint of 1814 edition)29 The book is available from our website: www.eschatology.org.

18. Thomas Ice and Kenneth Gentry, *The Great Tribulation: Past or Future?* A written debate. (Grand Rapids, Kregel, 1999)74+

19. Don K. Preston, *Israel 1948: Countdown To No Where*, 2002. The book can be purchased from our website www.eschatology.org

20. Merrill Unger, cited by Gentry, (*Tribulation*, 171)

21. Larry Spargimino, *The Anti-Prophets, The Challenge of Preterism*, (Oklahoma City, Hearthstone Publishing, 2000)194

22. I am convinced that the Song of Moses served as the blue-print for Paul's ministry. He saw himself as a last days prophet to Israel, destined to suffer martyrdom, "last of all" in the long march of the prophets sent to, and slain by, Israel. See 1 Corinthians 4:9, Colossians 1:24-26.

23. See my book *Who Is this Babylon?*, p. 30f, for a full discussion and demonstration of this important fact.

24. See my book *Have Heaven and Earth Passed Away?* Where I show that the Bible predictions of the destruction of "heaven and earth" refer to the destruction of Old Covenant Israel, and not the literal cosmos.

25. The book *Like Father Like Son: Coming on Clouds of Glory,* is now available on audio tape and CD. You can purchase the audio from our website: www.eschatology.org

26. Jack Van Impe, *Your Future: An A-Z Index to Prophecy,* (Troy, Michigan, Jack Van Impe Ministries, 1989)67

27. Thomas Ice, "The Seventy Weeks of Daniel 9" found at the website <<www.according2prophecy.org/seventy-weeks-pt1.html>>

28. In his written debate with Kenneth Gentry, *(The Great Tribulation*, Grand Rapids, Kregel, 1999)103), Ice, in a desperate attempt to negate Jesus' prediction that the end of the age would be in his generation (Matthew 24:34), argued, "The use of 'this generation' in all other contexts is *historical*, but 24:34 is *prophetic*. In fact, when one compares the historical use of 'this generation' at the beginning of the Olivet Discourse in Matthew 23:36 (which is an undisputed reference to A.D. 70) with the prophetic usage in 24:34, a contrast is obvious." Now, notice that he admits that 23:36 is an undisputed reference to A.D. 70. This means that the last days of Israel, per our argument, were undeniably in A.D. 70. Further, Ice's claim that Matthew 23:36 is a historical, and not prophetic reference is patently false. Jesus was *predicting* the events that were 40 years removed from him. To say this is a *historical* text, and not *prophetic*, is desperation exemplified.

29. Not only does Peter quote from Hosea, in v. 10, in verse 9 he quotes from Exodus 19:6, where Jehovah gathered Israel before Him at Sinai, and told them of His purpose for them. They refused to become what He desired, however. Peter is affirming in 1 Peter, that in Christ, Israel had finally become what God intended! I am currently working on an article showing that 1 Peter is an epistle fundamentally concerned with the "restoration of Israel." This flies in the face of many, if not most commentators, who feel that Peter was addressing a purely "Gentile audience."

30. The promise of the remarriage of Israel demands a transformation in the nature of the kingdom. Jehovah said Israel would fall "and never rise again" (Amos 5:1f), and that He was going to "bring an end" to the Northern Kingdom (Hosea 1:5f). In seeming contradiction, He then said He would marry her again in the last days. However, the solution is to remember that Israel was going to be *transformed* from the shadow to the reality, from the natural to the spiritual. God was indeed going to redeem Israel, but it would be through "judgment and through fire" (Isaiah 4:4), not through national restoration.

31. We plan to write a small book on this issue. The indisputable fact is that Paul was not just using "similar language" as Hosea, and he was not saying that his mission was a foretaste of the actual fulfillment of Hosea. He said his

mission was the fulfillment of Hosea's promise.

32. See my *Who Is This Babylon?* for a fuller discussion of the Wedding motif in scripture. Simply put, scripture knows of only *one wedding*, and that is of Israel. It is wrong to posit a wedding for Israel and one for the church, divorced (excuse the pun) from one another. This was what Jesus anticipated, Paul had initiated the betrothal, and John saw now perfected. What is often missed is that the Old Covenant form of Israel had to be removed so that the spiritual body of Israel, the remnant (the 144,000) would be the faithful and holy bride.

33. The millennialist assumes that the disciples still had the nationalistic kingdom in mind when they asked their question. This takes much for granted. If the disciples understood the nature of the kingdom in Acts 1 as they did earlier in Jesus' ministry, why did Jesus reject that kind of kingdom in John 6:15, and, importantly, why did Jesus have to open their eyes to understand the scriptures about that kingdom, and spend 40 days of intense instructions about it? The nationalistic kingdom was their heritage and history. They knew it well! Why would Jesus need to instruct them so intensely, and open their eyes to understand the kingdom if he was offering what they had known throughout their lives and history?

34. Arnold Fruchtenbaum PhD is cited extensively by Ice and other dispensationalists as a leading authority on prophecy. Ice sent me a three page article by Fruchtenbaum, entitled, "How the New Testament Uses the Old Testament." The quote comes from that article.

35. See my *Into All the World, Then Comes the End*, and *Who Is This Babylon?* for a fuller discussion of the Bible doctrine of the Coming of the Lord, judgment and resurrection. The book can be ordered from our website: www.eschatology.org.

36. See Bauer's, *Arndt and Gingrich Greek Lexicon*, (University of Chicago Press, 1979) 415

37. See for instance, Acts 16:1; 18:19, 24; 20:15; 21:7; 25:13; 27:12; 28:13

38. Dwight Pentecost, *Things To Come*, (Zondervan, 1966)134+

39. On one of his programs, Hagee said that if you did not believe that the Jews are still God's chosen people, then you are, "an intellectual air head." Jack Van Impe, attacking the position presented in this book, recently said preterists, "are full of more bologna than Oscar Meyer." I e-mailed Van Impe, four times, challenging him to meet me in public debate of this

issue. All I got in response was *a fund raising form letter telling me how much Mr. Van Impe appreciated my letter!*

40. An excellent new book by John Evans, *The Four Kingdoms of Daniel*, (Xulon Press, 2004), does a great job of debunking the liberal view of Daniel, and defending the "Roman View" of Daniel's vision. The book is available from our website: www.eschatology.org

41. Thomas Ice and Timothy Demy, *Fast Facts on Bible Prophecy*, (Eugene, Ore, Harvest House, 1997)158

42. See my comments in regard to the so-called Gap Theory of the millennial doctrine, in this book. The millennial Gap Theory is not only full of holes, it impugns the Deity of Jesus.

43. See my book *Seal Up Vision and Prophecy* for a full discussion of this important aspect of Daniel's prophecy. In a word, Daniel was told that by the end of the Seventy Weeks, the revelatory and prophetic process would be terminated, because all prophecy would be fulfilled. God's scheme of Redemption would be completed, and the need for prophet and prophecy terminated. The book can be ordered from our website: www.eschatology.org.

44. *Tribulation*, 115

45. Jack Van Impe, *Your Future: An A-Z Index to Prophecy,* (Troy, Michigan, Jack Van Impe Ministries, 1989)67

46. See my 2016 book, *The Resurrection of Daniel 12:2: Future of Fulfilled?* for one of the most exhaustive exegetical examinations of this prophecy to be found anywhere. The book can be purchased from Amazon, my websites and other retailers.

47. The LXX form of "the end" uses a form of the distinctive term used in Matthew 13. It is widely acknowledged that Daniel 12 is the source for Jesus' discussion of "the end."

48. John Calvin, *Calvin's Commentaries*, (Grand Rapids, AP and A, vol. 7)462

49. See my book *Who Is This Babylon?* for a more in-depth discussion of the language of Matthew 24:3.

50. It is an important fact of history that prior to the first century, the Jews simply referred to "the age to come." However, in the first century, they began to speak of "the age *about to come*," using the Greek word *mello* to emphasize the now imminent nature of the Age of Messiah. I am thankful to Ed Stevens for this historical fact.

51. The common belief among modern commentators is, as we have indicated, that the disciples were confused when they asked Jesus their questions. Commentators from millennialists to Postmillennialists agree, lamentably, on this one thing, the confusion or ignorance of the disciples. Yet, the disciples *said they understood Jesus' teaching about the end of the age in Matthew 13, and as we have seen, that involved the fall of Jerusalem.* Perhaps it is time to agree that it is the modern commentators that are confused, and not Jesus' disciples.

52. Please notice that the Hebrew writer does not say, contrary to many commentators today, that Jesus' death ended the Old Age. While Jesus' passion was doubtless the power that ultimately brought the Old World to an end, that Old World did not end at the moment of his death. It remained in place until the full end of the age which as we have shown in this work and others, occurred with the removal of the Temple. (See Hebrews 8:13; 9:6-10).

53. It should be noted that just because the OT says something is eternal, does not mean that it is *endless.* The Hebrew word *olam,* does not indicate endlessness, in and of itself. However, when things to end are contrasted with things that are *olam,* the idea takes on an enduring quality. In addition, when something is said to *never pass away,* the idea of endlessness comes into play (e.g. Isaiah 9:6-9).

54. It will of course be rejoined that 2 Peter 3 predicts the destruction of "heaven and earth." The problem is that Peter was discussing the Old World of Israel in typical apocalyptic and prophetic language that cannot be taken literally. I am currently revising my book *2 Peter 3: The Late Great Kingdom.* In that work, I show that the focus of Peter's epistle is the end of the Old World of Israel as foretold by the Old Testament prophets. Lord willing, the revision of that work will be finished in the not too distant future.

55. See, *The Destruction of Jerusalem,* by Holford. He documents from Bible and history that all of the signs given by Jesus did occur in the first century generation.

56. Ice claims that no false Messiahs appeared in the first century. He is wrong. Richard Horsley has documented the presence of many would be Messiahs in the days leading up to the fall of Jerusalem (Richard Horsley and John S. Hanson, *Bandits, Prophets and Messiahs*, (San Francisco, Harper and Row, 1985). Furthermore, Ice even admitted the presence of these false Messiahs in his debate with Gentry!

57. As a matter of record, LaHaye said that the generation that witnessed *WW I* would see the coming of the Lord. Tim LaHaye, *The Beginning of the End*, (Wheaton, Tyndale, 1972)165f. Later editions of this book omit the embarrassing earlier predictions.

58. Eusebius, *Ecclesiastical History*, Bk. III, chapter V (Grand Rapids, Baker, 1987)86

59. Hal Lindsay, 1980s: *Countdown to Armageddon,* (King of Prussia, Pennsylvania, 1980)117

60. See my work *How Is This Possible?* for a full discussion of this important text.

61. For a full demonstration that the Great Commission was fulfilled in the first century as Jesus promised, and the meaning of that fulfillment, see my book *Into All the World, Then Comes the End.* See the back cover for more details.

62. It is more than evident that, contra Jeffrey's contention, Ephraem did not hold the millennial view of "imminent but not near." He believed the end was truly near, and was to occur with the destruction of Rome, (not a *Revived* Roman empire). It is impossible to read his words and believe that he thought the end was to be delayed for 16 centuries.

63. Grant Jeffrey, *The Triumphant Return*, (Toronto, Frontier Research Publications, 2001)193

64. In fairness we must note that throughout church history, many believers, who were not dispensationalists, have foretold the end of the world for their generation. This sad history of failure haunts, or should haunt, the conscience of the church. For a historical review of failed doomsday movements, see Richard Abanes, *End Time Visions: The Doomsday Obsession,* (Nashville, Broadman and Holman, 1998)

65. Francis Gummerlock, *The Day and the Hour,* (Atlanta, Ga., American Vision, 2000)

66. Tim LaHaye and Thomas Ice, *The End Times Controversy* (Harvest House, Eugene, Or, 2003)85 This book is set forth by LaHaye and Ice as the definitive refutation of the preterist view. However, it is a shoddy piece of work that makes unsubstantiated claims and distorts the Biblical evidence in a shameful manner. The one thing that the book does do is to reveal how desperate LaHaye and Ice are to hold onto their preconceived theology...and their audience.

67. It is incredible to me that in a new book attempting to refute the ideas set forth in this book, one of the contributing authors, *who is not a dispensationalist*, takes the millennial approach to prophecy. Richard Pratt says "The historical contingency of human choice can make a difference in the way God fulfills a prophecy of judgment." *When Shall These Things Be?* Keith Mathison, ed. (New Jersey, P and R Publishing, 2004)128 What is so strange about this is that the editor, and many other contributors to the book, by and large categorically reject the dispensational view of a postponed kingdom. Yet, they have now adopted the millennial postponement paradigm!

68. Mark Hitchcock, *Second Coming of Babylon*, (Sisters, Ore, Multnomah, 2003)97)

69. J. N. Darby, *Lectures on the Second Coming*, (London, Paternoster, 1868)31.

70. Some will object noting that God promised to put the Messiah on the throne of David, and that this means God did intend to establish a national kingdom and literal king on the throne in Israel. This ignores the fact that David's throne for the Messiah was to be in *heaven*. In my upcoming book, *Like Father Like Son: Coming On Clouds of Glory*, I demonstrate that God's promise to enthrone Messiah was a promise to enthrone him in heaven.

71. Technically, Jesus did not come to fully establish the kingdom at his first coming. The full establishment of the kingdom is definitely posited for the *parousia*, or "Second Coming" (Matthew 16:27-28). Jesus declared that the kingdom was near (Mark 1:15), and, as it were, laid the foundation for the construction of the New Temple. The kingdom was "born" in infancy on Pentecost, nurtured by the Spirit for a generation of instruction and transition (Ephesians 4:8-16), and perfected by the *parousia* (Revelation 11:15f). The undeniable fact is that the kingdom was to be established in the first century, during the lifetime of Jesus' contemporary generation (Luke 21:28-32).

72. On our website, www.eschatology.org there are several articles dealing specifically with Paul, Israel and eschatology.

73. R. C. Sproul calls the evangelical community's attention to the problem of imminence language in the New Testament. Sproul correctly notes that the skeptical world continues to have a field day, discounting the validity of scripture due to the perceived *non-occurrence* of the "the end of the age has

come upon us" language. Sproul's appeal to take eschatology seriously needs to be heeded. R. C. Sproul, *The Last Days According to Jesus*, (Grand Rapids, Baker, 1998)

74. John Anderson and I are a co-signors of the *9.5 Theses for the Next Reformation*, drafted by John Noe and Ed Stevens. A copy of this Theses can be obtained from the International Preterist Association122 Seaward Ave. Bradford, Pa. 16701

75. John Anderson and I debated Thomas Ice and Mark Hitchcock, in October, 2003, at Christ's Covenant church in Tampa, Florida. Audio and video of that debate are available from my website: www.eschatology.org

76. Ice says that Zechariah 14 cannot be AD 70 because Jerusalem was destroyed not delivered. Of course Zechariah 14 speaks of both the destruction and deliverance of the City. Thus, Ice claims that the prophecy cannot refer to A.D. 70. What Ice fails to see is the doctrine of the Two Jerusalems. The Old Covenant city, the one that killed the Lord, would be destroyed (Zechariah 14:1-2), but the Heavenly Jerusalem, the one being persecuted, by the Old, would be delivered. See the development of this in my book *Who Is This Babylon?* Undeniably, the Bible has a doctrine of Two Jerusalems, one earthly, one heavenly. In prophecy, it is never the earthly city that is the focus of redemption and deliverance. The Old was but a shadow of "better things to come," and the better city is the body of Christ, the church (Hebrews 12:21f).

77. Ice claims that the "power of the holy people" of Daniel 12:7 is Israel's stubborn will, and that Daniel 12 will be fulfilled at the Second Coming at the end of the 7 year Tribulation. The trouble is that the Hebrew word translated as "power" Strong's #3027, is *never* used to speak of a stubborn will. Further, to suggest that Israel's rebellious heart is her "power, her strength" is to make *rebellion*, which is the same as witchcraft to God, to be a positive thing. Again, the word translated as power is never used in that sense.

78 Thomas Ice and Timothy Demy, *Fast Facts on Bible Prophecy*, (Eugene, Ore, Harvest House, 1997)158.

79 Josephus, *Antiquities of the Jews*, Bk. 6:3:4 and 3:7:7 (Peabody, Mass, Hendrickson, 1989) Updated version.

80 In his debate with Gentry, Ice appealed to Deuteronomy 4:25f as the roadmap of the future for Israel and said that Deuteronomy 28-30, specifically chapter 30:1-10, contains the prediction of a yet future return from captivity. Kenneth

Gentry and Thomas Ice, *The Great Tribulation* a written debate, (Grand Rapids, Kregel, 1999) 71+.The trouble is that Ice maintains that the Mosaic Covenant has been, "forever fulfilled and discontinued through Christ." (*Watch*, 258). It is patently illogical therefore, for Ice to affirm on the one hand that the Mosaic Covenant has been forever removed, and then *appeal to that abrogated covenant* as a roadmap of the future.

[81] Arnold Fruchtenbaum, in an article, "How the New Testament Uses the Old Testament," sent to me by Ice.

[82] I am currently writing a book, *Disciples of Denial*, chronicling some of the more glaring examples of how the millennialists blatantly deny the inspired statements of scripture. There are many passages in the NT in which the writers directly quote OT Kingdom prophecies and say that the church is "that which was spoken" by the OT prophets. In spite of these plain statements, our dispensational friends *deny* that the NT writers meant what they said. The dispensationalists are *Disciples of Denial*.

[83] We are not saying that the Day of the Lord foretold by Joel came on Pentecost. Joel spans the time "from Pentecost to Holocaust," as John Anderson likes to say. The events of Acts 2 were the initial acts of fulfillment, i.e. of the outpouring of the Spirit. However, as a result of the out pouring of the Spirit, signs and portents were to follow, and finally the Day of the Lord was to come.

Made in United States
Orlando, FL
24 January 2023

29008696R00085